THE BRITISH ECONOMY SINCE 1914

The British Economy Since 1914:
A Study in Decline?

REX POPE

LONGMAN
LONDON AND NEW YORK

Addison Wesley Longman Limited
Edinburgh Gate
Harlow, Essex CM20 2JE
United Kingdom
and Associated Companies throughout the world.

Published in the United States of America
by Addison Wesley Longman, New York

© Addison Wesley Longman Limited 1998

First published 1998

ISBN 0 582 301947 Paper

Visit Addison Wesley Longman on the world wide web
at http://www.awl-he.com

British Library Cataloguing-in-Publication Data

A catalogue record for this book is
available from the British Library

Library of Congress Cataloging-in-Publication Data

Pope, Rex.
    The British economy since 1914 : a study in decline? / Rex Pope
    p. cm. -- (Seminar studies in history)
    Includes bibliographical references and index.
    ISBN 0-582-30194-7
    1. Great Britain--Economic conditions--20th century.   I. Title.
II. Series
HC256.P66   1998
330.941--dc21   98–18329
                                                                CIP

Set by 7 in 10/12 Sabon
Printed in Malaysia, PP

CONTENTS

AN INTRODUCTION TO THE SERIES

Such is the pace of historical enquiry in the modern world that there is an ever-widening gap between the specialist article or monograph, incorporating the results of current research, and general surveys, which inevitably become out of date. *Seminar Studies in History* are designed to bridge this gap. The series was founded by Patrick Richardson in 1966 and his aim was to cover major themes in British, European and World history. Between 1980 and 1996 Roger Lockyer continued his work, before handing the editorship over to Clive Emsley and Gordon Martel. Clive Emsley is Professor of History at the Open University, while Gordon Martel is Professor of International History at the University of Northern British Columbia, Canada and Senior Research Fellow at De Montfort University.

All the books are written by experts in their field who are not only familiar with the latest research but have often contributed to it. They are frequently revised, in order to take account of new information and interpretations. They provide a selection of documents to illustrate major themes and provoke discussion, and also a guide to further reading. The aim of *Seminar Studies* is to clarify complex issues without over-simplifying them, and to stimulate readers into deepening their knowledge and understanding of major themes and topics.

ACKNOWLEDGEMENTS

I would like to take this opportunity to thank Tom Pope for his support in preparing the text of this book and also Gaynor Pope who, taking time off from her life's work of ensuring the prosperity of British car retailers, gave valuable help as an (unpaid) research assistant.

PUBLISHER'S ACKNOWLEDGEMENTS

The publishers would like to thank the following for permission to reproduce copyright material: Cambridge University Press for an extract from *English Culture and the Decline of the Industrial Spirit*, by M. Weiner 1981; two tables from *Dynamic Forces in Capitalist Development. A Long-Run Comparative View* by A. Maddison, 1991 by permission of Oxford University Press; *OECD Economic Surveys* for Great Britain. Copyright OECD 1979 and 1991; *The Sunday Telegraph* and Bill Jamieson for an extract taken from *The Sunday Telegraph* 3 August 1997; The Conservative Party for an extract from the 1983 Conservative Party Manifesto, *The Challenge of Our Times*; The Labour Party for an extract from the 1964 Labour Party Manifesto, *Let's Go with Labour for the New Britain*; The Liberal Party for an extract from *Liberal Industrial Enquiry, Britain's Industrial Future* published by Ernest Benn in 1928; an extract from *Britain and Europe* (1957) by The Economist Intelligence Unit Ltd. Reproduced by permission of the Economist Intelligence Unit Ltd.; The Centre for Policy Studies for an extract from *Solving the Union Problem is the Key to Britain's Recovery* by by Sir Keith Joseph 1979; The Policy Studies Institute for an extract from *Britain and World Trade* PEP June 1947; © *The Economist, London* for extracts from 11 January 1913, 31 January 1914, 15 February 1933 and 2 January 1937; an extract from *Fighting with Figures*, Office for National Statistics, © Crown Copyright 1995; an extract from *Economic Trends Annual Supplement 1996–97*, Office for National Statistics © Crown Copyright 1997; an extract from *Economic Trends*, Office for National Statistics © Crown Copyright 1997; extracts from *Technical Education*, Cmd 9703 © Crown Copyright 1956, the Dainton Report *Final Report into the Flow of Candidates in Science and Technology into Higher Education*, Cmnd 3541, © Crown Copyright 1968, an extract from the House of Commons Expenditure Committee, *The Motor Vehicle Industry: Report and Minutes of Evidence*, 617, 617/I-III, © Crown Copyright 1975 and an extract from the Wilson Report, Committee to Review the Functioning of Financial Institutions, Cmnd 7937, © Crown copyright 1980. Crown copyright is reproduced with the permission of the Controller of Her Majesty's Stationery Office.

Whilst every effort has been made to trace the owners of copyright material, in a few cases this has proved to be problematic and we take this opportunity to offer our apologies to any copyright holders whose rights we may have unwittingly infringed.

NOTE ON REFERENCING SYSTEM

Readers should note that numbers in square brackets [5] refer them to the corresponding entry in the Bibliography at the end of the book (specific page numbers are given in italics). A number in square brackets preceded by *Doc.* [*Doc.* 5] refers readers to the corresponding item in the Documents section which follows the main text. Words and abbreviations asterisked at first occurrence are defined in the Glossary.

ABBREVIATIONS

BMC	British Motor Corporation
BLMH	British Leyland Motor Holdings
CEB	Central Electricity Board
DfEE	Department for Education and Employment
EEC/EC	European Economic Community/European Community
ERM	Exchange Rate Mechanism
FCI	Finance Corporation for Industry
G7	Group of Seven
GDP	Gross Domestic Product
GEC	General Electric Company
GNP	Gross National Product
GNVQ	General National Vocational Qualification
ICFC	Industrial and Commercial Finance Corporation
ICI	Imperial Chemical Industries
IMF	International Monetary Fund
NEB	National Enterprise Board
NVQ	National Vocational Qualification
OECD	Organisation for Economic Co-operation and Development
OPEC	Organisation of Petroleum Exporting Countries
R&D	Research and Development
TEC	Training and Enterprise Council
TFP	Total Factor Productivity
TVEI	Technical and Vocational Education Initiative
VCT	Venture Capital Trust

PART ONE: THE BACKGROUND

1 INTRODUCTION

The title of this book suggests that there is a question as to whether the British economy since 1914 has been 'a study in decline'. This may seem surprising. Even before the First World War, deficiencies by comparison with the USA, Germany and other countries had been remarked upon. Since then, there has been the inter-war slump and, subsequently, the disappearance of much of Britain's traditional industrial base and a litany of criticism of this country's economic performance in relation to, first, the rest of western Europe and, more recently, countries on the Asian shores of the Pacific Ocean. Even the slightly more encouraging comparisons, with Europe at least, of the past decade have been seen in terms of a levelling down to Britain's standards.

But decline has only been comparative. It has not been all-embracing and uninterrupted. An index of Britain's Gross Domestic Product (GDP)*, taking 1990 as 100, shows a five-fold growth from 22.9 in 1913, to 36.9 by 1950, 72.2 by 1973 and 106.2 by 1995. Real personal disposable income per head roughly trebled during the post-Second World War period alone. Moreover, rates of economic growth have, for much of the twentieth century, compared favourably with those of other less criticised periods in the country's economic history. The nineteenth-century staple industries may have all but disappeared, but, at different times in the twentieth century, Britain has been the major European producer of motor vehicles, aircraft and even, if we discount the USSR, steel. Throughout the century, she has been a, if not the, major European centre for financial services and for a range of media-related industries [5, 44].

Thus, in examining Britain since 1914, we are not dealing with a moribund and internationally unimportant economy. Rather, we are looking at an economy which, in absolute terms, has performed better than ever before and one which contains centres of strength that are of immense significance in the 1990s. On the other hand, we are also examining an economy which fell from third to eleventh in terms of real GDP per capita between 1913 and 1979 and to seventeenth by 1994, and whose share of world exports of manufactures fell, between 1913 and 1979, from 31.8% to 9.7%. The purpose of this book is to analyse and explain *both* these aspects of Britain's history [30, 43].

MEASURES OF ECONOMIC PERFORMANCE

What should be taken into account in measuring Britain's economic performance? Overall economic growth rates (of Gross National Product (GNP)* or Gross Domestic Product) are an obvious starting point, though they have to be taken in comparison with Britain's historic record or the contemporary performance of other countries. However, the USA or Germany have much bigger populations than Great Britain in the twentieth century, while a country like Belgium has much fewer people. Thus, indicators of national income on a per capita basis are a valuable refinement. Another important measure of performance is productivity; what are the returns on given inputs of labour, capital or other factors of production and how do these compare with historic or other countries' figures?

Other matters might also be considered. The external balance of payments* and relative levels of inflation are examples of issues that can be seen as indicative of the health and expectations of the economy at a point in time. So too can the distribution of capital stock and the labour force or the make-up of production or sales. An over-commitment to goods or services for which demand is relatively stagnant or declining, e.g. shipbuilding, coal or cotton in the interwar economy, is ominous; an increasing presence in the world's major growth sectors, e.g. motor vehicles after the Second World War or media and communications in the late twentieth century, is encouraging.

One final point to consider is whether trends in growth or the balance of payments are the only or best indicators of economic wellbeing. The real income of individual members of the population is clearly another important measure of the national economic condition. Employment levels are too. Unemployment is not only a waste of a valuable resource but also excludes individuals and families from the benefits of economic advance. Assessment of an internationally healthy economic performance in the 1930s or the late 1980s or mid-1990s has to balance that against the historically high levels of unemployment in those periods; conversely the internationally poor performance of the 1950s and 1960s must be set against the high levels of employment enjoyed in that period. Finally, it might well be argued that the conditions in which people live are the ultimate test of a nation's economic state – not just material goods (including their housing) but also their health and the social and educational services and social security available to them.

MAIN ARGUMENTS

The overall debate about British economic performance in the twentieth century subsumes a number of important arguments concerning particular periods, sectors or contributions to that performance. The first issue concerns the starting point. Did the British economic position of 1913–14 contain fundamental if hidden structural weaknesses that ensured its subsequent decline, or might any problems have proved temporary and remediable had it not been for the intervention of the First World War? Should we, as economists of the 1920s and 1930s tended to do, blame the war for the loss of overseas markets and the consequent unemployment?

Interpretations of the inter-war economy are similarly varied. Traditionally, there was an emphasis on lost markets and the problems of the staple industries, compounded by the deep cyclical depressions of 1920–22 and 1929–32. Economic growth in the 1930s was no more than recovery from the world-wide slump at the beginning of the decade. Historians writing in the 1960s and after, using data not available earlier, have taken a more optimistic view. Some have stressed the period as one of economic innovation, one which saw the development of new areas of manufacture and service and which, in growth terms, compared well with pre-1914 experience. There has also been debate as to whether the 1920s or the 1930s saw the more impressive performance or whether achievement in the two decades was broadly similar. A further issue has been whether the economy of the inter-war years performed as well as that of the late nineteenth century. Another area of dispute concerns Britain's achievements compared to other countries in the 1930s. While a number of historians see this as one of perhaps only two periods during the twentieth century when the economy has performed relatively well, others (notably Alford) are sceptical, questioning the quality of the data available and the underlying strength of the 1930s upturn [25, 59].

Generally speaking, there is not a lot of disagreement concerning economic achievement during the period from 1939 to the beginning of the 1980s. Wartime organisation is generally praised but the potential for long-term damage acknowledged. While there is some criticism of government economic policy in the immediate post-war years, it is acknowledged that late-1940s difficulties were generally beyond British control. What was and is almost universally acknowledged and criticised is the lost ground of the ensuing decades. However, there has been disagreement as to the nature and causes of this. Some have criticised the performance of manufacturing industry, though opinions have differed as to whether this was the result of poor management and industrial relations, reflected in uncompetitive pricing or failings in quality, delivery or marketing, or the failure of banks and other financial agencies to support investment. Others have seen the problems as lying in the make-up of the British economy, with an over-commitment to slower growing sectors. Others, again, have seen difficulties as rooted in government action or inaction: 'stop–go' economic policies, high taxation, a heavy commitment to 'non-market' goods and services (in particular, welfare and military spending), lack of coherent economic planning and educational provision that was not geared to the needs of industry [Thatcher in 3, 14, 23].

The 1980s and 1990s are more controversial. Governments have emphasised these as decades of economic rebirth, the 'enterprise economy'. They have been characterised by wide cyclical swings, booms and slumps on a scale not experienced since the inter-war years and perhaps not even then. They have seen an accelerated decline in many sectors of British manufacturing and a great growth of financial services and industries based on media and leisure. During the latter part of the period, there have been occasions when Britain's unemployment and inflation rates, and sometimes even her economic growth rates, have compared favourably with those of other leading economies. The 1990s have seen huge inward investment. How to interpret this is a matter of lively debate and one not uninfluenced by the political persuasion of those concerned [6, 7].

Cutting across discussions about overall economic achievement are issues concerning sectors. This is apparent at the 'macro' level, e.g. the service sector as compared to manufacturing, or the 'micro', the relative performance of different industries. Does de-industrialisation matter if the services predominate in the world's dynamic economic sectors? Is non-European investment in British-based manufacturing desirable if it is, in substantial measure, the result of Britain being an economy with low labour costs? And within manufacturing, isn't the decline of some sectors (e.g. inter-war shipbuilding or cotton) and the rise of others (the manufacture of motor cars or artificial fibres) in the same period both historically inevitable and healthy? The only difference with past experience, and one which accentuates the price of mistakes and rewards of good decisions, is the ever-accelerating pace of change over the past 250 years.

There are major controversies concerning the role of governments in relation to the twentieth-century British economy. In the context of the period 1914–40, issues include the extent and pace of economic decontrol following the First World War, the deflationary policies associated with the return to gold in 1925, the failure to adopt Keynesian counter-cyclical policies in time of slump, the lack of commitment to regional regeneration and the overall contribution of the National governments of 1931–40 to the economic revival of that period. In relation to the period 1940–80, when Keynesian* principles of economic management were largely accepted, there are debates about the achievements in economic reconstruction from 1945 to 1950 and the effectiveness of government attempts to regulate the economy as a whole. There are also differing views concerning the impact of an increased commitment to social welfare on the resources available for investment in manufacturing or on the demand for goods and other services. Opinions also differ as to the potential and actual contribution of governments to the support and management of ailing industries (e.g. motor vehicles, shipbuilding) or to the encouragement and protection of areas of potential such as information technology. The relevance and usefulness of nationalisation or of heavy research investment in 'defence' industries provide further ground for dispute.

The years since 1980 provide a different agenda of issues. To what extent did government policies aggravate the problems of British entrepreneurs during the deep economic slumps of the early 1980s and 1990s? Have direct and indirect attacks on trade union power been instrumental in improving the efficiency of British industry and services? Have the incomes from North Sea oil and gas been used effectively? Has privatisation had a positive effect on economic performance of the sectors affected? Has there really been a retreat of government in matters economic?

Finally, there are issues, dating back to the later years of the nineteenth century, many of which might be described as essentially cultural. One is the extent to which any problems regarding overseas trade have been problems of marketing rather than problems of design, quality or price. Another concerns the scale of British overseas investment and whether this has diverted resources from home use. The relatively low status of economic activity and the lack of communication between political and economic elites, particularly in comparison with societies such as the USA or France, has also been offered as an explanation of Britain's relative economic decline. This has been linked to the supposed failings of Britain's schools and universities in respect of technological and commercial education.

Thus, whatever the assessment of British economic achievement during the period since 1914, that achievement and the reasons for it have certainly been centres of attention and debate. It is the intention in the remainder of this book to identify the essential elements of the different arguments and to evaluate the points made, to demonstrate that the nature and focus of any criticism has varied over time and, finally, to offer a summary comment on how British economic performance might be judged [55].

PART TWO:
THE BRITISH ECONOMY SINCE 1914

2 STILL COMPETITIVE: THE BRITISH ECONOMY IN 1914

On the eve of the First World War, Britain was one of the world's three great economies. She was no longer the 'workshop of the world'. The USA and Germany were forging ahead in industrial production. But Britain, as the greatest trading and financial power, remained at the centre of the international economy. Moreover, there was optimism that the under-achievements and threats of the last quarter of the nineteenth century had been overcome and that a new era of competitiveness, expansion and prosperity could be expected [*Doc. 1*].

At one time, economic historians tended to concentrate their attention on the so-called 'Great Depression' of 1874–96 and dealt with the Edwardian period mainly in the context of the ongoing problems of particular industries, notably iron and steel. With the arrival of revisionist assessments, offering more positive views of entrepreneurship and economic performance in the late Victorian period, came greater attention to the beginning of the twentieth century. These have, however, had to sit beside calculations which suggest that the turn of the century saw a decline in the rate of economic expansion with GDP growing at 2.0% a year from 1856 to 1899 but only 1.1% a year between 1899 and 1913. During the past ten years or so, debates have continued, with contributors to the Elbaum and Lazonick collection emphasising failure while others suggested a more cautious assessment of cause, if not of overall record [33, 42, Floud in 72].

All historians accept that the pace of growth of the British economy, which had been slowing since the mid-nineteenth century if not earlier, declined further in the period 1900–07 (but also that it showed a slight recovery in the years 1907–13). They agree, too, that Britain's rate of economic growth in the late nineteenth and early twentieth centuries was slower, in per capita as well as absolute terms, than that of major rivals like Germany and the USA. There is also general acceptance that British investment in producers' equipment was lower as a percentage of GDP than that of her two main rivals. However, they disagree about the significance of this situation and about its causes [Floud in 72, 78].

BRITISH INDUSTRIES IN 1914

Arguments about the state of the economy in 1914 turn on the performance of the great staple industries, Britain's showing in new and generally science-based industries and the impact of overseas investments on overall economic performance. Discussion here will be limited to four staples (steel, cotton, coal and shipbuilding) and three 'new' industries (electrical engineering, motor vehicles and chemicals). It is recognised that various other branches of engineering or major sectors like wool textiles or agriculture might, equally appropriately, have been selected.

The steel industry, a staple industry but also one in which science played an important part, has often been singled out as an exemplar of British economic decline. From a position of supremacy in the 1870s, British output had fallen far behind that of the USA or Germany. Over the five years 1910–14, British annual output averaged some 7 million tons while that of Germany averaged 15 million and that of the USA 27 million. An increasing proportion of British steel was produced by the open hearth method, which provided better quality control than the Bessemer process, but a majority of the output remained acid steel, requiring ores that were low in phosphoric content. US and German producers benefited from home markets that were protected by tariffs. A guaranteed home market, especially one dominated by huge corporations like US Steel or cartels*, encouraged investment in large-scale integrated plant utilising the latest technology. Such plant gave US and German producers a competitive edge in other markets, including Britain itself.

The British industry, by contrast, comprised modest-sized family firms, lacking the capital resources or the market to justify investment in the latest, implicitly large-scale and integrated plant. Its major products, ships' plates (which took 42% of the British open hearth steel), sheet steel and tin plate were at the specialist, high-quality end of the market. Producers of ships' plates, by forming associations and giving rebates to shipbuilders who used exclusively British steel, had been able to drive out foreign competition. However, by 1913 there were significant imports of steel plate for non-shipbuilding purposes.

Circumstances which added to uncompetitiveness included a wage structure which protected firms with low productivity, and, because of the concentration on acid steels, the increasing cost of home and overseas supplies of low phosphoric haematite ores as these became depleted. The German industry, with a concentration on basic steels, thus secured a further competitive advantage.

The British steel industry undoubtedly contained many firms that were competitive and it successfully withstood competition in its major home markets. Nonetheless, its international competitiveness was impaired by its atomised structure, its exclusion through tariffs from the most dynamic of world markets, its concentration on acid rather than basic steels and therefore its vulnerability to higher ore costs, and a wage structure that did not encourage increased productivity [76, Sandberg in 35].

Contemporaries were less concerned about the condition of other staple industries, and historians, though divided, have been similarly, on balance, a little more positive. There was no doubt that, in coal output, Britain had been overtaken by the USA, and that output per man year, having peaked at 319 tons in the 1880s, had fallen to an average of 257 tons for the years 1908–13. However, stagnation or decline in labour output was a characteristic of all European countries, a consequence, more than anything else, of the exhaustion of better or more easily worked seams. As a result, British labour productivity in 1913 remained on a par with that of Germany and rather better than that of France or Belgium. Continued increase in US output per man reflected that country's enormous reserves, in generally shallower and thicker seams.

Lack of investment in mechanised coal-cutting and underground haulage has also been proposed as a symptom of British inefficiency. By 1913, only 8.2% of British coal was cut mechanically and a rather smaller proportion removed from the face using electrically powered conveyors. However, the Belgian figure for machine-cut coal was only marginally better at 10% and that of the Ruhr a mere 2%. British coal-mining was not under-capitalised at this time in relation to that of the USA, though much of British investment related to the much greater average depth of pits, and lack of mechanisation underground was in part due to geological factors. Nor, with output rising 27.6% between 1900 and 1913 to 287 million tons, 97 million tons of which was exported (much of it as bunker coal), and coal accounting for some 5% of UK national income in the early years of the century, did there appear to be cause for concern [31, 76, 106].

The state of the cotton industry appeared to contemporaries to be similarly healthy. The industry expanded rapidly in the decade before 1914, increasing the number of spindles and looms by nearly a quarter while continuing to make modest gains in efficiency and maintaining its position of hegemony in the manufacture and export of cotton. Britain had 40% of the world's spinning and doubling spindles and a third of its power looms. Overseas sales constituted a quarter of the value of all British exports with 86% of piece goods produced exported in 1912. Increasingly, though, these exports were to less developed countries, notably India. On the eve of the First World War, that country was taking more than 50% by value of all British grey cloth, 20–30% of bleached and 10–15% of dyed. This huge dependence on exports to a single market of a product whose manufacture demanded relatively low levels of technology was a source of vulnerability for the industry [Lazonick in 33, 118, 120].

Other potential sources of competitive weakness were the industry's limited adoption of new technologies and its internal organisation. On the technological side, British firms had been slow to adopt either ring spinning (introduced in the 1860s and 1870s) or the Northrop automatic loom, introduced in the 1890s. By 1913, just 19% of British-spindles were rings, compared to 87% of American, and 1–2% of looms automatic, compared to 40% in the USA. However, this situation has been seen as economically rational. Ring spinning saved money in America where it used an unskilled labour force, largely female, rather than skilled male spinners. This offset the extra costs resulting from the need to use longer staple and usually more expensive cotton, except at the very lowest counts (fine-ness) of yarn. In Britain, a ready supply of skilled mule spinners reduced the ring's advantages in labour costs. Thus, while rings were generally adopted for lower counts, for higher counts (above 40) manufacturers, as in France and Germany, kept to mule spinning [108, 120]. Automatic looms reduced labour costs by enabling the operative to control more looms. Against that, they were more expensive than the traditional Lancashire loom. In the USA, labour savings outweighed the additional cost of installing automatics; in Britain, they generally did not.

However, although entrepreneurs appeared to be making economically rational decisions, the widespread introduction of new textile technologies elsewhere in the world did have an effect on Britain's relative position. In particular, ring spinning reduced the longstanding advantage in human capital that Britain held in its mule spinners. It can also be argued that sticking with mules and Lancashire looms thwarted moves towards greater overall efficiency and competitiveness. The industry remained competitive, in the face of increased demand for low-price and low-quality goods, by reducing the quality and quantity of raw cotton inputs to the production of yarn and cloth. This strategy and the principal means by which it was achieved, increased sizing of the warp yarn (i.e. coating it for strengthening), was technically more feasible using existing production methods. However, this technologically conservative response to market conditions, along with the multi-layered and generally fragmented structure of the industry, was to be a cause of longer-term difficulties. Economies of vertical* and horizontal* integration, and high throughput, were not widely adopted in Lancashire. While this was undoubtedly the case, two points have to be emphasised. Lancashire had structure, buildings, technology and an abundant labour force in place. Entrepreneurial decisions were made in this context. Also, the industry had secured and was maintaining an overwhelming domination of the world's cotton trade; Lancashire's cotton industry was not failing before 1914. Moreover, the most commonly cited exemplar of modern capital intensive practices, the Massachusetts cotton industry, was to face difficulties every bit as great as those of Lancashire in the inter-war years. Thus, the problems of Britain's cotton industry were not self-evidently the result of poor decision-making in the pre-1914 era [Lazonick in 33, 120].

Contemporary and historical judgements of the different sectors of the engineering industry varied but there was, and has been, little criticism of the performance of British shipbuilders. Although other countries, including the USA and Germany, were developing their shipbuilding capacity, protected by tariffs, British yards were still responsible for 60% of the merchant tonnage produced between 1900 and 1910. This achievement was assisted in no small way by the fact that Britain controlled 35% of the world's shipping fleet [*Doc.* 2].

Like most other sections of the British economy, shipbuilding was characterised by relatively small family firms and a strong dependence on skilled workers. In 1910, the total output of 1,134,000 tons was the product of 85 firms and 91 shipyards; most firms were, therefore, single yard operations. The development of steam-powered metal ships, and of increasingly sophisticated vessels, especially in the warship and liner sections of the industry, had led to a proliferation of shipbuilding crafts. In the early twentieth century, shipbuilding was unique among major sectors in having over 60% of its workforce classified as skilled.

The industry was strongly unionised with tight control of entry, demarcation and manning levels. This organisation was of use to employers in respect of transmission of skills, while the widespread practice of subcontracting particular tasks to squads of men reduced the need for supervisory management. Local union branches also operated as a form of labour exchange and, by providing unemployment or sickness benefit in time of hardship, helped maintain a supply of appropriately skilled labour.

The high degree of specialisation of the British workforce coincided with a heavy concentration of shipyards on certain rivers, e.g. the Wear, the Tyne or the Clyde. This allowed workers to move from yard to yard according to where work was available. Thus employers benefited from a highly skilled workforce which could be hired or laid off as required. Overseas competitors rarely enjoyed this situation and had, therefore, to give more continuity of employment to a workforce with less specialised skills.

Mechanisation of the yards was limited. Useful riveting and caulking machines, utilising pneumatic power in what were non-skilled processes, were only introduced from the turn of the century. Machine tools had to be flexible, able to produce components of differing sizes, and mobile and overhead cranes were only used in the larger liner or warship yards, such as Harland and Wolff in Belfast or Swan Hunter and Wigham Richardson on the Tyne. UK yards, therefore, by restricting their fixed capital investment, further enhanced their competitiveness in an industry where, liners and warships apart, demand was acutely sensitive to fluctuations in economic conditions.

Thus, strong national demand, geographical location, workforce organisation and flexible costs combined to create an industry which remained clearly superior to any of its international competitors in the period up to 1914 [Lorenz and Wilkinson in 33, 115, 112].

The record in newly developing engineering sectors was less impressive. In electrical engineering, British firms led the world in cable manufacture. In more technologically sophisticated areas, such as lamps, telephones, heavy machinery or electrical traction, other countries were well ahead. Indeed, there was considerable penetration of the British market by German and American firms in some areas. This was the sort of science-based industrial activity where deficiencies in Britain's education system may well have had an influence. Another factor was probably the nature of the existing industrial base. There were limited advantages in introducing electrical drive to sectors such as textiles; moreover Britain's steam engineers offered highly developed and efficient equipment. Limited utilisation of electrical goods was reflected in the power generated. Britain's 1914 output of 3.0 gigawatt hours (gwh), while second greatest in Europe, lagged far behind the German figure of 8.8 gwh [44, Pollard in 72] [*Doc. 3*].

Motor vehicle manufacture was another industry slow to develop in Britain. Indeed, the commercial manufacture in Britain of motor vehicles started only in 1896. However, by 1913, British output, enhanced by Model T Fords assembled from 1911 at Trafford Park using American kits, at 34,000 cars and commercial vehicles was rapidly catching up with that of France (45,000). Both, though, were dwarfed by US production which was more than four times that of Europe.

British firms were pioneers in the production of pressed steel bodies and of chassis frames. Some, e.g. Humber, also adopted the specialised machine tools, flow-through assembly lines and use of semi- or unskilled labour on repetitive processes which characterised the successful cycle industry. Final assembly, however, remained basically craft practice with a good deal of hand-fitting and finishing. The emphasis on quality and high technical specification, producing a variety of cars for the better off, was characteristic too of French manufacturers who, by virtue of their earlier start, had established a considerable export trade to Britain, the main European market for motor vehicles by 1914 [32, 107].

The real contrast in productivity and in manufacturing and marketing techniques was with the USA. While much of the contrast in this respect has been ascribed to weak management and a low-wage industry with low capital-labour ratios (seen as consequences of social tensions emanating from British economic decline), the real explanation would appear to lie in the size of the internal markets. The huge capital investment needed to establish the special-purpose machinery, interchangeable parts and moving assembly lines that went with a disciplined and highly paid workforce was only practicable in the context of economies of scale from large volume output. In 1913, Ford of America produced more than 200,000 vehicles; the largest French producer, Peugeot, produced 5,000 and the largest British manufacturer (if we exclude the kit-assembled Fords), Wolseley, 3,000.

On the eve of the First World War, there were signs of change. Ford cars with their high horse-power but slow engine speed did not need the precision machining of parts necessary in British engines with their higher engine running speeds. Moreover the cars, thanks to imported American parts and the efficiency of the Trafford Park plant, were cheap, the Model T runabout costing £135. Among British manufacturers, a newcomer, Morris, broke with British practice, assembling cars entirely from parts produced to contract by specialised suppliers. But the Morris Oxford (1912), which retained the typical British highly efficient, low horse-power, high speed engine, still cost £175, 30% more than the cheapest Ford. Plans to produce the cheaper Cowley, utilising components imported from American suppliers, were interrupted by the outbreak of war. By 1913, Ford's sales of more than 7,000 Model Ts represented some 60% of the British market for cars priced at under £200 [Lewchuk in 33, 107]. The position of the British chemical industries again demonstrated the tendency to lag behind rivals in more science-based activities. The late nineteenth century saw rapid growth in employment in this sector, and in soaps, paints, explosives or coal tar intermediates, Britain was the equal of any country. But in high growth, newer chemicals, such as dyes, drugs, photographic chemicals or electrochemicals, Germany or the USA was far ahead and the overall output of those countries dwarfed that of Britain. In 1913, while Britain produced 11% of the world's chemicals output, Germany produced 24% and the USA 34%. Much has been made of the delay, by British firms, in switching from the Leblanc to the Solvay process in soda-making or from lead chamber to contact process in the manufacture of sulphuric acid. Quantitative analysis suggests that the economic case for an early switch may have been over-stated. Nevertheless, British research and development failed to keep up with that of Germany, particularly in respect of pharmaceuticals and dyestuffs. These areas, then as now, were research-intensive and the Germans benefited from their education system and the large supply of scientists it produced. Once behind, it became increasingly difficult to catch up. Indeed, it has been suggested that it was sound short-term decision-making on the part of British firms to limit their activities in this area [Sandberg in 35, 116, Vol. 1].

OVERSEAS TRADE AND INVESTMENT

Though overtaken in industrial production, Britain remained the major trading nation (and, linked to this, the greatest provider of shipping) and was still, overwhelmingly, the hub of the international financial market and the main source of international investment. Overseas investment in 1914 has been estimated at some £4,114 million, 44% of the world total. The holdings of the next three largest investors (France with 19.9%, Germany with 12.8% and the USA with 7.7%), taken together, amounted to less than the British figure. In addition, British investment was spread world-wide, whereas much of the US commitment was to Central and South America, and some 50% of that of France and Germany was to central and eastern Europe including Russia. Moreover, investment by the other European powers was closely linked to the development of markets for their industrial products, whereas British investment, nearly half of which in the period 1900–13 was in transportation, was geared more to increasing world trade in food and raw materials, supporting the development of the British economy in a less direct way [25, 48, 71]. The economic effect of this overseas investment has long been an issue of dispute among economists and historians. The high level of capital exports (5.3% of GNP 1900–14) was in the context of low gross national capital formation. Contemporaries like Hobson saw overseas investment as being at the price of a more even distribution of wealth in the UK, which would have been to the benefit of the poor and of industry alike. Others emphasised the benefits that additional overseas investment brought to British industry, services or infrastructure. Bankers and financiers at the time argued that overseas dividends increased the demand for goods and services at home. In truth, it is hard to argue that high overseas investment had any directly deleterious effect on the domestic economy. There is no evidence of entrepreneurs or public authorities being the victims of capital starvation. Indeed, economic opinion in recent times has tended to minimise the importance of those traditional inputs to the economy, capital and labour. Much more importance is assigned to what used to be known as the residual, that part of economic growth which is left when the effects of additional labour or capital are removed. This Total Factor Productivity (TFP)* includes a number of non-quantifiable inputs, not only technical change but also improvements in human capital (physical or mental), in labour organisation, in industrial relations, changes in government policy etc. Capital investment may depend on other variables or may change in harmony with them. It is not a condition of growth. In fact, low domestic investment in the years leading up to the First World War could be seen as a consequence of poor economic performance, not a cause of it [25, 42].

CONCLUSION

Overall, it would be wrong to condemn British economic performance on the eve of the First World War. Much of any lost ground was inevitable given the near hegemonic position the country had enjoyed in the mid-nineteenth century and the sheer scale of resources available to major competitors like the USA or Germany. It was true that the country lagged behind in a number of newer, high technology sectors, but in several important cases this was to prove a temporary phenomenon. There is a tendency, too, to concentrate on a limited number of economic activities that take place in international markets. A balanced assessment of Britain's 1914 economy would need to take into account goods and services provided largely or exclusively for the home market. Another tendency is always to compare British performance with best practice overseas; other countries also had examples of poor management practices, less than optimum use of labour, sectors that performed disappointingly. There is also a danger of judging with hindsight. It was reasonable, in the context of pre-war trading performance, for the British government to resist calls for protection. Similarly, it was reasonable for manufacturers with buoyant order books to stick with existing markets and methods of production. The historical judgement may be that there was a long-term price to be paid for such decisions, but it does not follow that they were wrong at the time.

3   PAINFUL ADJUSTMENT, 1914–1939

During the period 1914–39, there was clear evidence of absolute decline in the output of a number of staple industries and of an overall national economic performance that compared poorly with that of other countries during the 1920s. On the other hand, 'new' and service industries, mainly serving the home market, expanded substantially, and during the 1930s the British economy appeared to perform better than that of competitor nations. Historians have debated a number of issues concerning these developments. Were the problems of staple industries inevitable, caused or exacerbated by the 'Great War', or did they result from entrepreneurial or managerial weakness? How impressive was the performance of 'new' industries; could it have been better? How should overall economic growth be rated? To what extent did government policies, on debt reduction, returning to and subsequently abandoning the gold standard, tariffs and any industrial strategy, contribute to the overall picture?

EFFECTS OF THE FIRST WORLD WAR

The First World War came upon a country and an economy unprepared for war and with no experience of a conflict between industrialised powers. Much is made of an initial call for 'business as usual' and of both the inappropriateness of such an objective and its incompatibility with mass mobilisation of long duration which Kitchener, Minister for War 1914–16, recognised as necessary. The war brought initial disruption and unemployment. Over time, however, demand for labour, including that of women, built up as an increased demand for armaments and other war supplies coincided with the diversion of millions of young men into the armed forces. Overseas trade was reduced, disadvantaging some major exporters but giving opportunities in areas where imports had been significant. While luxury trades suffered and many small firms were forced out of business, the profits of others were greatly boosted by the demands of war.

In the long term, the war probably hastened but did not cause the decline of the staple industries which had formed the basis of nineteenth-century prosperity. It also encouraged the development of newer industries. Some have argued that the war itself offered opportunities for economic re-organisation which were ignored at lasting cost. This, in the context of the economic priorities and constraints of wartime, is somewhat fanciful. What can be said is that between 1914 and 1918, as between 1939 and 1945, the British economy's performance and management compared favourably with those of other major combatant powers, and that in the immediate aftermath of war Britain's economy was in better shape than that of most of her European neighbours [25].

Though exports declined, war did not harm the older staple industries in the short term. Cotton fared well during and immediately after the war, albeit at considerable long-term cost. Shipping shortages and government quotas reduced the supply of raw cotton and increased its price, but demand for yarn and cloth (including from governments for war-related purposes) drove up the price of the finished product. In spite of severely reduced exports, profit margins reached unprecedented levels. Between 1912, itself a fair year, and the early months of 1920, there was a 36-fold increase in the profit to be made on a standard count American yarn and a 12-fold increase in the profit on shirting made from the same yarn. These inflated profits did not, as in past booms, lead to a substantial increase in new buildings and equipment. The building and textile machinery firms, themselves disrupted by war and faced with buoyant demand, could not have responded quickly enough. Instead, in 1919–20, there was an orgy of speculation with 49% of the spinning section (mostly producing American yarn) and 14% of weaving firms financially reconstituted to the short-term profit of the shareholders and the banks. At the same time, war had accelerated the development of overseas cotton manufacture, particularly in Lancashire's Far Eastern markets [4, 117, 118].

Coal-mining and iron and steel met home demand by diverting exports. In the case of coal, output declined by some 50 million tons between 1913 and 1918, largely due to lost manpower. The industry became progressively more controlled by government and this control (nationalisation) remained in place during the immediate post-war years when industrial demand and the disruption of western European supplies kept prices high. However, war had caused the loss of some overseas markets while output had been maintained by the working of more accessible seams. Thus the industry was ill-prepared for the harsher economic climate of the 1920s [47, 106, 124].

War demands meant government-sponsored development of the iron and steel industry. Steel-making capacity rose by some 50% to 12 million tons. Further commitment to the basic steel-making process allowed for increased use of scrap and waste in production and there were improvements in plant efficiency, in the ability to produce to specification. The war also stimulated research and development in areas such as alloys or tool steel manufacture. Unfortunately, much of the increased steel-making capacity only became available in 1919–20 and it was more than matched by similar developments elsewhere in the world (US output also increased by 50%, a further 15 million tons). Moreover, new British plant was largely in the form of extensions to existing works; it was not linked to shifting production to areas of lower cost. The period 1920–33 was to be one of acute world over-capacity with British producers operating at little over half capacity [Tolliday in 33, 47, Warren in 65].

In shipbuilding, too, the war led to a substantial increase in British and world capacity and the rise of competitors, with the USA briefly becoming the leading shipbuilder. The number of British berths rose from 580 in 1914 to 806 in 1920. Once again, peak output only came after the war was over. In 1920, 5.9 million tons of shipping were launched, 35% of this (2.1 million tons) by British yards. The needs of warships led to the widespread introduction of welding to replace riveting, a change which was also apparent in merchant ship construction. Overall, though, changes were limited with additional capacity being developed on conventional lines in association with existing yards [47, Parkinson in 65, 112].

The chemical industries were among those which gained most as a result of the war. The explosives sector's gains were, in part, short-term but the need for toluene for TNT stimulated the establishment of a British petro-chemical industry. Ammonium nitrate was also in great demand for explosives. Brunner, Mond and Co. were encouraged to develop new production methods, while in 1918 the government began work on a new nitrogen fixation plant at Billingham. The end of the war led to the sale of this plant and 'all relevant information' (including that gained post-war from the German firm, BASF) to Brunner, Mond. War needs proved the catalyst in switching to the contact method in the production of sulphuric acid and to the development of cellulose acetate production for use in doping aircraft wings or in manufacturing window substitutes for battle zones.

Loss of imports from Germany and other continental countries forced the rapid development of British dyestuffs, where government funding aided the establishment of the British Dyestuffs Corporation and Scottish Dyers Ltd in 1919 (to merge in 1925). Pharmaceuticals and margarine manufacture also benefited from the reduction in overseas supplies. Sales of soaps gained from the wartime rise in real incomes. Though much of the European market was closed to British firms, removal of competition meant increased opportunities for sales elsewhere in the world, especially the USA. Wartime experience also led to amalgamations. Chemical companies, internationally, were large-scale and capital-intensive. British firms, to compete, needed to be similar in size and resources. The war saw Brunner, Mond absorb rivals in alkali manufacture and the amalgamation of different explosives firms into Nobel Industries in 1918 [Timmins and Pope in 49, 114, 116 Vol.1].

The war also affected motor vehicle manufacturing in a positive way, although there is room for debate as to the extent of the benefits incurred. In the short term, private motoring was reduced, petrol supplies were restricted and productive capacity was diverted to munitions work. Against that, military demands and dilution agreements encouraged increased use of standardised jigs and the subdivision of production processes, leading to unskilled labour replacing semi-skilled on what often proved to be a permanent basis. War contracts allowed a firm like Morris to double the size of its Cowley plant and build up both the workforce and the number of sub-contractors supplying parts. The introduction of a 33⅓% protective tariff on cars and components, initially under the McKenna Duties (1915) but retained almost without a break for nearly 50 years, not only assisted British car manufacturers but also persuaded Ford to use British components. It is possible to exaggerate the innovations and lessons of war or the value of greatly expanded factories that had been geared to the manufacture of planes, armoured vehicles and the like in relatively limited runs. Nonetheless, the balance was one of clear advantage for the long-term development of the motor vehicle industry [107].

The electrical engineering and supply industries were probably handicapped, on balance, by circumstances associated with the war. The electrical supply industry lost key men and found equipment manufacturers transferring production to more profitable war work. Increased demand for power did lead to the establishment of a Department of Electrical Power Supply in 1916 and sales of electrical energy did increase from 3.0 gwh in 1914 to 4.9 in 1918. Wartime measures were, though, devised to meet short-term demand. Plant installed had low optimum generating levels and was often ill-located; tight government controls also inhibited the development of the industry [25, 44].

As we have seen, however profitable industries were, war had severely affected exports. By 1918, the volume of domestic exports had been reduced to 40% of their 1913 level and by 1924 had only recovered to 80% of the earlier figure. In the Far East, especially, markets had been lost to Japanese and Indian producers. By value, however, they reached 2½ times the 1913 figure in 1920, at the peak of the inflationary boom, and remained at 1½ times 1913 values in 1924 [25, 44].

The impact of the war on British financial holdings and the balance of payments was significant without being disastrous. War requirements forced the sale of some assets and capital holdings declined by a quarter at most during the war years. There was disruption of international financial markets through the payment of war debts and reparations. Devaluation of sterling and loss of shipping earnings (more competition and a particularly marked decline in the volume of British trade) were further causes of a deteriorating performance. City of London institutions, where war not only affected financial confidence but also speeded the rise of rival markets, notably New York, also contributed less than pre-war. Overall, net invisible income fell by between a quarter and a third in real terms between 1913 and 1920, while between 1913 and 1924 the gap between Britain's invisible trade* surplus and her visible trade* deficit was halved [25].

During the inter-war period, there was a tendency to blame many of Britain's economic difficulties on the war of 1914–18 and its effects. In the early 1920s, this was linked to an optimism that the problem was a temporary one and that the prosperity associated with the old economic order would return. In fact, the war's effects varied by sector but should not be over-emphasised. In the case of staple industries like coal or cotton, the war did not create but did vastly accelerate the development of overseas competition and did not allow a managed adjustment to new market conditions. A similar argument might be put forward regarding city financial institutions. In steel-making and shipbuilding, war encouraged some technological adjustment but a premium on short-term increases in production rather than long-term planning meant that war demands tended to inhibit rather than stimulate technological or organisational advance. It also generated a world-wide over-capacity which affected British plant like that of other countries. For other sectors of the economy, war proved a long-term stimulus. This included sections of the chemical industries and electrical engineering where freedom from German supplies and competition necessitated the development of British production. The emerging British industry benefited from a change in government policy regarding protection, a change which also had significance for British motor vehicle manufacture. However, here too there is evidence of a longer-term trend; this was an industry where Britain was already gaining on the leading European producer, France, in the years before the war. Protection of nascent or strategic industries, like government-funded research or assisted investment, might be interpreted as positive consequences of war-induced government action. The politics of economic decontrol in 1919–20 and the ensuing inflationary boom and the return to the gold standard* in 1925 were, and are, frequently interpreted as examples of war-related government actions that were less than helpful to the British economy.

THE 1920s AND 1930s: GENERAL PERFORMANCE

Britain, between the wars, was a country of economic contrasts. After short-lived post-war prosperity (1919–20), traditional staple industries, including cotton, coal-mining, iron and steel manufacture and shipbuilding, experienced acute difficulties, particularly in export markets. The problems of these industries were reflected in closed mills, works, mines and shipyards and lasting, large-scale regional unemployment, particularly in the north and west. In addition, economic performance as a whole was seriously affected by the deep cyclical slumps of 1920–22 and 1929–32, throwing additional millions out of work. Against this, several industries and services supplying the home market achieved modest prosperity during the 1920s, suffered only to a limited extent during the general economic downturns and expanded strongly during the years after 1932, creating new jobs as they did so, mainly in the south-east and midlands [*Doc. 10*].

In this context, a number of issues of debate have emerged among economic historians. Overall, there is the question of what growth rates were and how these can be compared with those of other countries at the time or historical British rates. Government policy has also been an issue. Were the difficulties of exporting industries exacerbated by policies associated with the return to gold in 1925? Conversely, to what extent did selective protection during the 1920s assist the development of particular industries and a wider range of measures under National governments in the 1930s contribute to a more broad-based recovery from slump? With regard to particular industries, there are issues as to how far the problems of the staples were inevitable or manageable and how to judge the performance of apparently more successful sectors.

Measuring overall and comparative rates of economic growth for inter-war Britain is particularly difficult. Statistical data varies in quality and content from country to country and even over the two decades for Britain itself. In particular, there is a tendency towards double counting where manufacturing work is sub-contracted. This has the effect of exaggerating fluctuations in growth rates. Above all, varying rates of recovery by countries after the First World War, and sharp but far from uniform downturns in economic activity in the early 1920s and 1930s, mean that the choice of base years can have a substantial impact on overall findings [59].

In considering British overall economic performance, Dowie's choice of 1924, 1929 and 1937, all years at the peak of an economic cycle, is probably the soundest approach. He calculates that, between 1924 and 1937, GDP grew at 2.3% p.a., with more or less equal performance 1924–29 and 1929–37, while industrial production excluding building grew at 3.0% and output of manufacturing alone by 3.3%. This compared favourably with the 1.1% p.a. of the period 1900–13 and is not dissimilar to rates in the second half of the nineteenth century, 2.2% during the so-called 'Victorian boom' of 1856–73 and 2.0% over the longer time-span 1856–99. However, there were contrasts between the two inter-war sub-periods. In that of 1929–37, growth was actually concentrated in the period 1932–37 when GDP grew at a rate of nearly 4% p.a. Growth rates in manufacturing and distribution accelerated in the 1930s, offsetting deceleration elsewhere in the economy. Labour productivity, as measured in output per man year, was some 50% higher in the 1930s compared to the 1920s. Though many so-called new industries were to the fore in terms of productivity gains, they were in the company of others such as textiles or agriculture where there was substantial shedding of labour [24, 42, 59, 68].

International comparisons show Britain performing relatively badly over the period 1913–29 with an increase in GDP of 0.7% p.a., markedly worse than that of any other major economic power [*Doc. 11*]. Even taking the years 1922–38, thereby eliminating the effects of Britain's particularly deep post-war slump, shows a weaker performance, 2.1% p.a. compared to an average of 2.6% for ten European economies. The 1929–38 performance was much better. Britain averaged 1.9% p.a. growth, only bettered by Germany and the Scandinavian countries. Growth in GDP per man year (1.0%) lagged behind that of all major competitors when measured over the period 1924–37, while calculations for 1913–29 (1.5% p.a.) and even 1929–38 (0.9% p.a.), based on hours worked, show Britain as lagging behind all but Germany in the former period and all important economic rivals in the latter. By the end of the period, British GDP per person hour stood at $4.97 (in 1985 $US), an increase of about one-third on the 1913 figure. Only the USA, at $7.81, out-performed the UK, but the figures for France ($4.25) and, to a lesser extent, Germany ($3.57) were converging on those of the UK [25, 41, Eichengreen in 72].

'OLD' AND 'NEW' INDUSTRIES

It is, by now, widely acknowledged that a division between 'old' industries that declined and 'new' industries that thrived in the inter-war period is too simplistic. Some 'old' industries, or parts of them, were favoured by, or adapted to, conditions, especially in the 1930s. Not all 'new' industries were successful. Overall, though, it was the great staple industries, most heavily dependent on export markets, that faced the greatest difficulties during the years 1919–39.

In terms of output growth over the whole inter-war period, it might be argued that the British steel industry performed relatively well. While European output increased by 36.5% between 1913 and 1936–37 and that of Germany by 36.4% to 19.5 million tons, British output grew by 61.5% to 12.6 million tons. The 1930s saw considerable rationalisation of the industry, including amalgamations and the closure of redundant plant; per capita output levels in 1937 were nearly twice what they had been in 1923.

The 1920s were, however, bleak years for the British steel industry. War-driven expansion in capacity, generally on old sites and using outdated organisation and technologies, was not needed in the depressed trading conditions that followed. Exports, affected by protective tariffs, competition from reconstructed continental works and, in some cases, British companies establishing plant overseas, averaged 3.5 million tons a year between 1919 and 1929, 19% less than in the decade 1903–13. At home, low levels of shipbuilding, ship repair and marine engineering (which had taken 30% of ingot production in 1913) caused particular difficulties. Nor was there sufficient compensating growth in the demand for lighter steels. As late as 1937, steel for cars, bicycles and aircraft made up just 7% of British production, whereas in the USA, automobile steel had become the leading sector. Moreover, the market was regionally divided and, within regions, there was a lack of industrial concentration as well as diverse product demand (Tolliday in 33, Warren in 65).

Market difficulties led to under-use of plant. In the period 1921–33, utilisation was rarely over 60% and fell to 30% in 1921 and 1927. This added to the costs of production and reduced both the incentive and capacity for modernisation. Problems were compounded by the fragmentation of the industry and of its products. The top ten firms were responsible for just over half the output of the industry in 1920 and just over two-thirds by 1937. Furnace and overall works size, though increasing, was small by international standards, hot metal practice was rare and production of basic steel, while doubling between 1914 and 1925 to two-thirds of British output, still fell below optimum levels and had not been accompanied by appropriate relocation. As a result, high rail freight charges added to the difficulties of British steelmakers.

A protective tariff of 33⅓% from 1932 was conditional on extensive rationalisation and reconstruction. It coincided with a booming demand for consumer products, for constructional steel and, later, for armaments. There were significant amalgamations. In Scotland, Colvilles established a near monopoly in heavy steelmaking; Richard Thomas took over a number of other firms in the South Wales tinplate and sheet steel industry. The establishment of English Steel (1929) and Lancashire Steel (1930) involved significant plant closures. Some integrated plant, notably that of Stewarts and Lloyds at Corby, achieved world-class standards of efficiency. Richard Thomas built a continuous strip mill at Ebbw Vale on the US model. There was some rationalisation of location; both Scunthorpe (responsible for over 10% of British steel output by 1937) and Corby used cheap local Jurassic ores.

But rationalisation did not go as far as it might have done. Ebbw Vale was a poor site for a strip mill. There was a general neglect of tidewater facilities, important in an industry where transport constituted a significant element in costings. Much of the rationalisation, especially that of Colvilles in Scotland, involved on-site improvement of existing works rather than creation of integrated plant with the latest in ancillary technologies. As a result, efficiency gains were limited. Nor was the British Iron and Steel Federation, working from 1934 in collaboration with the government's Import Duties Advisory Committee to promote modernisation and re-organisation, especially successful. Divided by inter-company disputes, it curbed competition and contributed to a rationalisation less radical than was necessary for the long-term prosperity of the industry or was practicable given the protected market and buoyant demand of the 1930s [Tolliday in 33, Warren in 65].

The experience of the British coal-mining industry was worse. By 1937, output was 40 million tons down on 1913. Three-quarters of the decline was due to lost exports. Growth in the world capacity to supply coal, a product of new major producers and increased mechanisation of the pits, coincided with increased protection of home markets, greater fuel efficiency and the development of substitute fuels. The industry's problems were compounded by the difficulties of major coal users, notably iron and steel manufacturers, railways and shipping. World demand for coal had risen by some 4% a year before 1914 but grew by only 0.3% a year during the inter-war years. Britain's share of world production was reduced from 25% to 20% and, whereas by 1937 European coal-mining output was 25% above the 1909–13 average, that of Britain was still 10% down.

To an extent, this absolute and relative decline was unavoidable. In coal, as in other products, Britain had depended heavily on export markets. However, during and immediately after the war, domestic needs had taken priority and the quantity available for sale overseas had been restricted. Countries, including Holland and Russia, that had been significant pre-war markets for British coal increased home production, thereby permanently reducing their demand for the British product. Stagnation in the British shipping industry and the transition from steamships to motor vessels were also important. In 1913, 97% of the world's merchant shipping (44 million tons) was coal-fired; by 1937 the figure was 49% (32 million tons). Use of British bunker coal fell from 21 million tons to 12 million in the same period [106, 124].

Changing production techniques and increased fuel efficiency hit home markets. Between 1920/21 and 1934/35, the electricity supply industry achieved economies in the use of coal and coke of the order of 55%, while the period 1913–36 saw economies of 20% in the amount of coal required to produce a ton of pig iron. The demands of the iron and steel industry were affected not only by fuel efficiency but by the increased use of scrap in steel manufacture. A 40% increase in steel output (1920–37) led to no increase in the use of pig iron and therefore coal; by the end of the period, scrap accounted for nearly 60% of the tonnage of steel ingots produced [106].

Overall, however, domestic demand for coal in 1937 was comparable to that of 1913, with increased use in electricity generation offsetting losses in other sectors of the market. The problems of the industry, so far as sales were concerned, were essentially export-based.

The industry also lost ground to continental rivals, as well as the

Americans, in mechanised coal-cutting and underground haulage. In 1913, Britain compared favourably with the Ruhr, Belgium and France in terms of percentages of coal mechanically cut. However, by 1929 the continental fields could claim 72–91% but Britain only 28% mechanically cut. By 1936, the figures were 88–97% for the continental fields and 55% for Britain. In underground haulage, Britain lagged even further behind. However, as with mechanised cutting, lack of investment and technological innovation stemmed in large measure from lack of necessity.

Output per manshift was higher in Britain in 1913 than in the three continental areas identified. The major reason for this was relative ease of underground conveyance. By 1937, although the increases in labour productivity had been much more marked in the other fields, only the Ruhr, where underground conditions were comparable with those in much of Britain, had achieved greater output per man shift. Even so, other countries were making significant gains in terms of wage costs per ton of coal and this, along with intervention by foreign governments, made the British product less competitive. While the average price of British exported coal rose by some 30% between 1929 and 1938, that of Germany or Poland fell by 38% and 33% respectively.

Government intervention, in the form of the Coal Mines Act (1930), created compulsory owners' cartels to establish output quotas and fix minimum prices for different grades of coal as well as a Reorganisation Commission to oversee amalgamations. The quota and pricing system was used by the owners to protect the inefficient and possibly to slow the adjustment to market conditions. At best, the Act had a neutral effect on the industry with inhibitions to change counter-balanced by amalgamations and rationalisation encouraged by the experience of the cartels [105, 106, 111].

By 1938, output at 227 million tons was some 16% down on the average for 1909–13. Whether or not the 1930 Act had helped or hindered rationalisation, the inter-war years had seen a substantial number of amalgamations and pit closures. By 1938, the 2,125 mines in operation represented a fall of over a thousand compared to 1909–13, and the workforce, at 790,900, had declined by nearly 280,000. Nonetheless, the industry retained many inefficient units and there was substantial scope for further reorganisation [106].

Between 1913 and 1937, world consumption of cotton goods rose by 36% but international trade in the commodity fell by 38%. Piece goods (woven cloth) constituted the lion's share of this trade. During the 1920s, the volume of British cotton piece goods exports averaged

58% of their 1913 level; by 1935–39 they averaged no more than a quarter. Given the hegemonic position enjoyed by the Lancashire cotton industry before 1914 and its dependence on exports, the sharp decline in international trade was bound to have a severe effect. Lancashire's problems in world markets were exacerbated by her concentration on the Far East trade. Here, aided by the interruption of supplies between 1914 and 1918, Indian, Japanese and Chinese mill production expanded to meet the demands of their home markets and to compete for exports. Protective tariffs encouraged this process; on the eve of the Second World War, India's mills supplied 86% of the sub-continent's home demand while Japanese imports accounted for 8% and British imports only 4% [Lazonick in 33, Porter in 65].

Lancashire's reaction to difficult markets was constrained by her industrial inheritance. An abundance of existing mills, machinery and labour encouraged a conservative response. Old buildings (most Lancashire mills dated from the nineteenth century) were deemed unsuitable for automatic looms. By 1939, no more than 5% of looms were automatics; in the USA the figure was 95%. Some 28% of spindles were rings; the US figure was 99%. American and Japanese manufacturers sought to maximise their use of plant by shift-working and concentration on long runs of a limited and standardised range of yarns or cloths. In Lancashire, operative resistance to shift-working meant that most mills ran for just 48 hours a week while continuing the pre-1914 practice of switching between a wide variety of yarn counts or cloths as a means of staying in business. Electric drive, better lighting and improved mill lay-out gave further advantages to overseas producers in modern mills. One economist suggested that, in the 1930s, output per man-hour in the American cotton industry was 100% greater than that in Britain [21, Porter in 65] [*Doc. 7*].

A more positive response, and one which demonstrates the limitations of an 'old' industry/'new' industry approach to analysis of inter-war performance, was adoption of artificial fibre, generally rayon, a product of the chemicals industry. Much of the output was a mixed cotton-rayon product, leading to gains in quality and appearance. By the end of the 1930s, some 20% of looms in operation were producing cloth incorporating some artificial fibre [Harrop in 65].

Rationalisation of capacity was left initially to industry initiatives such as the bank-supported Lancashire Cotton Corporation or Combined Egyptian Mills. Only in 1936 did government intervene with the Cotton Industry (Reorganisation) Act, establishing a levy-based Spindles Board to purchase and scrap 10 million surplus spindles. By the outbreak of war, it was half way to its target. Ironically, over the period 1929–38 the weaving section, where there was no government intervention, was more successful than spinning in reducing capacity; numbers of looms fell by 37.7% compared to 30.4% for spindles. In spite of rationalisation, the movement into mixed fibres and economic recovery, the industry was still operating at a quarter to one-third below capacity by 1938. As elsewhere, the efforts of government or the industry had been insufficient [24].

UK shipbuilders were affected by a world excess of shipping in relation to trade where only in 1929 and 1937 did demand approach the tonnage available. Their prosperity, or lack of it, was particularly linked to the demands of British shipowners. There was a natural tendency to turn to home yards, though in 1938 100,000 tons of shipping were built in German yards for British owners, while overseas sales were inhibited by foreign governments' protection policies. Competitiveness in difficult markets was not helped by weak management (there was little attempt to modify working practices) and by intensification of demarcation of function within the workforce. In comparison to those in Holland or Germany, UK yards were undercapitalised and there was less attention to material flows or the organisation of production. One writer has calculated that there was little or no improvement in productivity in the industry between the pre-First World War years and the late 1930s [Parkinson in 65].

Output fell. UK yards launched over a million tons of new ships in all but two years of the period 1920–1930, but following a collapse to 133,000 tons in 1933 they only achieved a million tons in one year (1937) during the 1930s. The country had quickly regained its position as the world's major shipbuilder but was producing generally less than 40% of total tonnage in the 1930s, compared to over 50% between 1927 and 1930 and over 60% before the First World War.

Government intervention tended to be piecemeal and could hardly be described as policy. Shipbuilding gained substantial loan guarantees under Trade Facilities Acts during the 1920s, subsidies under the not very successful 'scrap and build' scheme of 1935 and, in the case of John Brown's yard on Clydeside, benefited from a low-interest loan of £8 million to Cunard to build the two Queens for the transatlantic liner trade. Re-armament in the 1930s was a boost to the naval sector [Parkinson in 65, 112].

Electrical engineering was a successful 'new' industry. Its growth record, averaging 4.7% a year from 1920 to 1938, was second only to that of motor vehicle manufacture. The industry had been stimulated by war, both in terms of technical advance and in terms of range and quantity of output. In the 1920s and 1930s, it was to benefit from rising real incomes, new products, increased availability of hire or hire purchase facilities and, above all, a vast improvement in the public electricity supply.

At the beginning of the inter-war period and throughout the 1920s, Britain lagged behind other major economic powers in total and per capita consumption of electricity. However, following the establishment of the Central Electricity Board (CEB) and the commencement of the National Grid, consumption in Britain rose rapidly. Between 1929 and 1935, it expanded by 70% in the context of world growth of only 20%. By 1939, per capita consumption had overtaken that of Germany and Italy, caught that of France and was closing on that of the USA. Though variations in voltage, type of current and price remained, the CEB and Grid, coupled with sound business decisions on the part of most major producers (commonly local authorities), did bring about widespread standardisation and cheaper prices. The result, aided by the availability of credit or hire arrangements for those wishing to wire their homes and by the construction of large numbers of new, ready-wired houses, was a belated growth in the mass market. The 730,000 consumers of 1919 and 2.8 million of 1929 had become nearly 9 million by 1938.

Cables, which represented over a quarter of output by value in 1924, suffered from difficult export markets and fell to under 16% by 1935. Electrical machinery and parts held their position with 21–22% in both 1924 and 1937. British companies in this sector also caught and overtook foreign rivals in the production of high capacity and high voltage equipment. The real growth was in electrical consumer durables, predominantly for the home market. These accounted for under a quarter of output value in 1924 but their share rose to over 38% by 1937 when wireless apparatus alone contributed just over 12%.

The wireless industry had been stimulated by the First World War but major manufacturers built on this, forming the British Broadcasting Company in 1922 to stimulate demand for their products. The Marconi company was free in its allocation of patent licences (2,200 by 1929). The dull emitter valve, coupled with mass production and fierce competition, led to the development of smaller and cheaper sets. The £30 cost of a set capable of receiving all European stations in 1920 had been succeeded by sets priced at £6 to £8 by the late 1930s. Market penetration was eased by finance houses' provision of hire purchase facilities. By the late 1930s, some 2 million radios and radiograms were being sold every year.

Other relatively cheap electrical goods to have found mass markets by the end of the 1930s included vacuum cleaners (400–500,000 sold in 1939, three-quarters of these on hire purchase) and electric irons (sales of 1.5 million in 1939). Permeation of the market was less impressive with more expensive and heavier users of electricity such as cookers (1.5 million in use and sales of 220,000 in 1939), wash boilers or water heaters. Here, customer inertia appears to have been reinforced by the higher purchase costs of such items [Catterall in 65, 103].

There were limits to achievements. Although competition squeezed out some wireless manufacturers in the 1930s, a number of relatively small firms remained, many simply assembling parts made by others. Such firms did not undertake research and this, perhaps, was one reason why the British wireless manufacturers tended to follow the technological lead of the Americans. Moreover, in the 1930s, output per worker in the US radio industry was more than four times that in Britain. American radios were, in consequence, both cheaper and more sophisticated than those made in Britain. Overall, though, the British electrical engineering industry had done some catching up. Before the First World War, the British industry, much of which comprised offshoots of American or German firms, had been seen as lying 'a poor third' to those of Germany and the USA, with generally unsophisticated products. By the end of the inter-war period, though Britain remained third, her products were more diversified, she was closer to Germany and the USA in terms of export performance and, in spite of continued American influence, there was much less dependence on foreign-owned firms [Catterall in 65].

A 'new' industry which has attracted much debate concerning its inter-war performance is that of motor vehicle manufacture. Output of cars stood at 116,600 in 1924 (second in Europe to France with 145,000), at 179,200 in 1929 and, recovering strongly after a slight fall during the depression of 1929–32, at 379,300 in 1937. By this time, Britain was, by a margin, the biggest European manufacturer, with Germany (276,600) in second place. Exports, at 15,700 in 1924, 34,000 in 1929 (in both cases figures for all motor vehicles) and 65,000 (cars alone) in 1936, showed a similar move from being second to France in the 1920s to market leader in the 1930s, with Germany second by the end of that decade [104].

A number of factors contributed to relative success in comparison with the rest of Europe. Protection, except for a brief spell in 1925, remained at the 33⅓% level imposed in the McKenna Duties and, from 1926, was extended to commercial vehicles. Capie has argued that the effect of tariffs on this sector was greater than that on any other industry. Certainly, it offered protection of a home market where, although motoring taxation was relatively onerous, average real wages were appreciably higher than in France or Germany, car prices were slightly lower, running costs appreciably lower (mainly due to the price of petrol which, in 1937, stood at 19.5p per gallon in Britain but 25.6p in France and 34.7p in Germany) and hire purchase facilities were more developed [66, 104, 107].

Criticism of Britain's motor vehicle industry centres on comparisons with the USA and on the extent to which opportunities for greater growth and production efficiencies were not taken. Lewchuck, in particular, while acknowledging major British vehicle makers' use of flow production, drew attention to the high proportions of profit absorbed by dividends and to low levels of capital investment. In the 1930s, Austin was utilising £175–200 of fixed capital per worker; Ford of Detroit had been using $5,500 per worker in 1921. One consequence was the high average price of British cars in relation to American, £210 compared to £159.30 in 1936. This, he argued, held down demand [Lewchuk in 33].

It is certainly true that British firms were less efficient than American but there were other reasons for smaller output and sales. The size and purchasing power of the American population created a scale of demand for a standardised mass-produced vehicle that made large-scale capital investment, on Fordist lines, an economically rational approach to manufacture. In European countries, with their smaller populations and income distributions that restricted inter-war car purchase to the middle and upper classes, such policies were inappropriate. Firms like Berliet or Citroen in France, or Fiat in Italy, which tried them, came close to financial disaster. British firms could certainly have improved on their production processes, and the presence of six major producers, and the consequent range of product lines, also reduced efficiency and raised prices. However, the historically useful comparison for the 1920s and 1930s is with the rest of Europe, not with the very different situation in the USA. Using that measurement, the British industry performed relatively well [104, 107].

For the most part, British chemical industries, with developing sectors protected under the Dyestuffs (Import Regulation) Act (1920) or the Safeguarding of Industries Act (1921), did well in the inter-war period, though this was not necessarily a product of sound judgement. Imperial Chemical Industries (ICI), a merger of Brunner Mond, Nobel Industries, the United Alkali Company and the British Dyestuffs Corporation, was formed in 1926. Size and areas of expertise allowed it to participate in technical exchanges and market-sharing agreements with the other major companies of the world, notably I. G. Farben and the US firms Du Pont and Allied Chemical and Dye. Other British chemicals firms, while smaller than ICI, were far from insignificant and in some cases, e.g. Distillers, Courtaulds or Unilever, were also parts of powerful combines. Indeed, Distillers and Courtaulds led the way in developing products based on organic synthesis. ICI's record was, in fact, patchy. An always risky £20 million investment at Billingham to develop production of ammonium sulphate for fertiliser was followed by the 1929–32 slump in agricultural prices and a decision to run the plant at half the planned capacity. In the 1930s, the major commitment was to the production of petrol by hydrogenation of coal. Both ventures diverted energies and capital from potentially more profitable activities.

Overall, though, the late 1930s saw the chemical industries in a healthy state. Production of synthetic fibres, dominated by Courtaulds and British Celanese, grew from under 6 million metric tons at the beginning of the 1920s to over 60 million by the late 1930s, though this growth had been far surpassed by that in Germany and Italy. Output of synthetic dyestuffs had risen from 5,000 tons in 1913 to 29,000 in 1937, with protection ensuring that imports were only half the level of exports. Production of synthetic pharmaceuticals had also grown strongly, as had that of celluloid or bakelite, solvents and soap powders. Nonetheless, traditional heavy inorganic production still predominated and the main developments in petro-chemicals still lay in the future [44, Harrop in 65, 116, Vols 1 & 2].

There was at the time, and has been since, some criticism of Britain's record in research and development (R&D), especially in science-based growth sectors. Certainly, evidence from major firms in the chemicals and electrical engineering industries suggest American levels of R&D investment in the late 1930s of up to ten times those of Britain. However, the comparison between Germany and Britain is less clear. I. G. Farben spent more than ICI but the German firm's work was more diversified, covering research in areas like pharmaceuticals, synthetic rubber, fibres and photography which was undertaken by other major British companies. By contrast, British electrical engineering firms employed more researchers than their German rivals. Overall, British and German industrial research, at least early in the decade, seems to have been at comparable levels, but well below that of the USA [69].

THE RETURN TO GOLD AND OTHER GOVERNMENT ACTIONS

There has been wide support for the view that British under-achievement in the 1920s was, in part, a consequence of the decision to return to a gold standard with a fixed rate of exchange at the pre-1914 level of $4.86 to the pound. Nominally, Britain had remained on gold throughout the war. In 1919 the position was abandoned since, at that time, the deflationary actions required to stay on the standard were politically unacceptable. This was, however, considered a temporary measure, and from 1920 steps were taken to restore the value of the pound and allow re-establishment of the gold standard and the fixed exchange rate. These steps were necessarily deflationary, compounding the effects of the slump of 1920–22 and the increase in labour costs that had resulted from an increase in institutionalised wage-bargaining and a sharp reduction in working hours. Moreover, once the gold standard had been restored, in 1925, further deflationary measures were necessary in the form of high interest rates to maintain the value of the pound, whilst the $4.86 decided upon increased the burden of debt repayment, a significant issue for post-First World War governments, and with it taxation [63, 80] [*Doc. 6*].

Criticism, at the time and since, has centred on the rate of exchange rather than the principle of a return to gold. While some have seen both as putting the interests of the city before those of industry, a country as dependent as Britain on external trade, both visible and invisible, benefited from the re-establishment of order in world financial markets represented by the return to the gold standard. The main disputes have centred on the effects of the $4.86 exchange rate, seen by Keynes at the time as a 10% over-valuation. This has been blamed for making exports less competitive in what were already very difficult world markets and for permitting other countries, following Britain in the return to gold, to engage in competitive rate-fixing [59, 80] [*Doc. 4*].

While generally accepting that the pound was over-valued (though stressing the importance of effective as opposed to nominal over-valuation), a number of economic historians have questioned whether this had any significant effect on 1920s economic performance. Some have emphasised the fact that nearly half of British exports went to countries in the sterling area* and thus were not affected by over-valuation, though this argument seems to ignore the impact of competition within the sterling area from countries outside it. More pertinently, the problems of Britain's traditional exporters were centred on changes in world demand, growth in competition or relative inefficiencies; 10% lower prices in the late 1920s would not have restored their markets. Nor is it reasonable to argue that other countries would not have devalued their currencies in relation to the pound had Britain not adopted a high rate of exchange. In an age of political attention to comparative economic advantage, it is likely that the governments of countries like France or Belgium would have sought a competitive rate whatever the level chosen by the British [25, 59, Sayers in 80].

On balance, it would seem that the return to gold has been made a scapegoat for Britain's relative economic failure in the 1920s. It is probably true that the interests of the financial markets shaped the original decision and that the important invisibles sector in British overseas trade benefited from the higher rate selected. Visible exports were probably not substantially affected; market conditions (including the re-entry of Germany into world markets) and internal inefficiencies were much more important. Deflationary measures taken to restore and then maintain the value of sterling depressed home demand and slowed the development of consumer durable and service sectors. However, a feature of the 1919–20 boom was excessive investment in old technologies and industrial sectors and thus government policies may be held to have prevented further misallocation of economic resources.

Government policy, though more limited in scope than some contemporary commentators would have wished [*Doc. 9*], has sometimes been seen in a more positive light in respect of protection and policy initiatives during the 1930s, including abandoning the gold bullion standard and establishing low interest rates.

Selective protective tariffs, imposed during the First World War, had been maintained during the 1920s. Thus motor vehicle manufacture remained subject to protection. Another war measure, retained under the Dyestuffs (Import Regulation) Act of 1920, placed a ten-year ban on the import of dyestuffs, except under licence. The Safeguarding of Industries Act (1921) not only replaced the wartime licensing arrangement by a 33⅓% duty on other 'key industries', including certain chemicals and magnetos, but also allowed similar protection in the event of dumping or the depreciation of a foreign currency. Some of these measures lapsed, others were reinforced during the 1920s, but there was no resort to general protection and at the beginning of the 1930s more than four-fifths of imports were still allowed in free [47, 66].

A policy of general protection followed the abandonment of the gold standard in September 1931. Emergency legislation allowed duties of up to 100% to head off a feared flood of imports. In early 1932, under the Import Duties Act, these duties were replaced by a general tariff of 10% on all imports except those, including important raw materials and foodstuffs, on a free list. Following a review by the Import Duties Advisory Committee, a general tariff of 20% on manufactured goods was introduced in April 1932. In particular cases, the rate was higher, notably steel where the duty was set at 33⅓% in 1933 (and even at 50% temporarily in 1935). Initially, these duties did not apply to empire products. The Ottawa Agreements (1932) confirmed the principle of imperial preference with Britain gaining tariff concessions from the Dominions in return for admitting most of their goods free and imposing additional duties, and later quota restrictions, on some competing foreign imports [25, 66].

Tariffs were generally highest on imports from Europe. There was also an upward drift in the levels of duty during the 1930s. They were used, as bargaining tools, by the government in a series of bi-lateral trade agreements, notably that with the USA in 1938.

The consequences of tariffs are difficult to measure. The effect on imports depended not only on the level of duty but on elasticity of demand and on decisions by the seller; in some cases the effect of the duty imposed was nullified by a reduction in the selling price. The effective rate of protection (the margin of protection on value added in production) was probably more significant than the nominal rate and the textile industries were better served in this respect than iron and steel, shipbuilding or some of the so-called new industries. Exports may have been adversely affected through concentration on the domestic market, through depressed overseas purchasing power, through the imposition of retaliatory duties or, in instances where manufactures utilised taxed imports, a rise in costs and prices and, consequently, reduced competitiveness. Conversely, they may have benefited from economies of scale possible given the protected home market or as a consequence of bi-lateral deals [24, 25, 66, 67].

Was British economic performance boosted by the various forms of protection in place during the 1920s and 1930s? Certainly, the 1931–32 tariffs were accompanied by a decline of 44% in retained imports. Exports, by contrast, remained stable. Imports did, though, grow rapidly during the recovery phase of the economic cycle, 1932–37. However, by 1937 manufactured imports, in spite of some dumping, were still 17.6% below their 1929 peak during a period in which

GDP had risen by 17.0% and industrial production by 30%. Export volumes, faced by higher tariffs, also rose after 1932 but failed to approach their 1929 levels; moreover adverse movements in the terms of trade led to a deterioration in the trade balance. Tariffs almost certainly played a large part in the sharp decline in imports from 1931 to 1933. There were also clear long-term benefits to industries like motor vehicle manufacture or some chemical sectors, with an almost uninterrupted high level of protection from 1915. Nor can we ignore the potential consequences of not adopting tariffs. What would have happened to British manufacturing had this country remained the only important unprotected market? [*Doc. 8*].

Overall, tariffs appear to have had a marginally beneficial effect during the inter-war period, but a precise measure of their impact is impossible and, in assessing government policy in relation to economic performance, it is legitimate to ask whether more protection at an earlier date might not have had a positive effect [25, 66, 67].

In fact, as its timing indicates, the introduction of general protection in the 1930s was not aimed primarily at curbing imports, rather at checking the fall in the pound following the abandonment of gold. This it did and with the Exchange Equalisation Account (established in 1932) operating to avoid wide fluctuations in the value of sterling, the pound eventually stabilised at a shade above its previous dollar level. Abandonment of the gold bullion standard and the initial depreciation of sterling was forced on the government in the context of the 1931 financial crisis. A new equilibrium was established between currencies, though it should be stressed that some, notably the yen, depreciated in relation to the pound at this time and others, including the dollar and major European currencies, later. While the pound's controlled float did not hinder export recovery after 1932, it is difficult to argue that it was a major contributor to it. International trade did not regain the levels of the late 1920s and Britain's share of that trade diminished still further [25, 73].

With confidence in the pound restored and domestic interest rates insulated from those abroad, the National government relaxed monetary policy. Bank rate, at 6% in September 1931, had fallen to 2% by the end of June 1932. It was to stay at this level until the end of 1938. Cheap money enabled the government and many industrial borrowers to reduce the burden of debt servicing, but bank lending fell until 1936, and even by 1938 only construction, entertainment trades and professional and private lending stood at a higher level than in 1929. Growing manufacturing sectors appear to have relied on undistributed profits, and to a lesser extent on new share issues, rather than on bank advances which, at around 4.5%, were hardly cheaper than in the 1920s. Cheap money did, however, contribute, along with changes in mortgage lending practice and lower building costs, to the private sector housing boom of 1932–39. During this period, investment in private sector homes represented over half of all building investment and over a quarter of total gross domestic investment [24, 43].

THE ROLE OF THE BANKS

The role of the banks in relation to British industry was criticised at the time and has been since. The 1931 Report of the Macmillan Committee on Finance and Industry compared British banks' reluctance to lend to small and medium-sized companies with the more positive role of banks elsewhere, including Germany and the USA. In fact, the Bank of England and leading commercial banks did become heavily involved in the affairs of particular industries, including cotton, steel and motor vehicles and through the establishment of the Securities Management Trust or the Bankers' Industrial Development Corporation. It is also true that British banks, by avoiding rash investment, proved more stable than their German and US counterparts and that this benefited the economy. However, much of the involvement was with larger companies, and loans tended to be short-term. It was also the case that British banks utilised 1930s prosperity to increase liquidity. Even the more interventionist role of the Bank of England can be seen as essentially defensive and temporary, to avoid political interference in the banking sector provoked by economic crisis [26, 81].

CONCLUSION

On the eve of the First World War, Britain, while a world leader in many important areas of economic activity, did appear to be slow in developing high value-added technologically advanced industries. With the help of the war and a more interventionist government stance, the national position in sectors such as chemicals, electrical engineering and motor vehicle manufacture had all improved by 1939. So too had the relative position in steelmaking. By contrast, the position of some traditional leading sectors, including coal-mining, textile manufacture (especially cotton), textile engineering and shipbuilding, had markedly deteriorated. Yet these industries remained among the, if not the, biggest in the world, and, in capital and employment numbers, dwarfed most of the so-called 'new' industries. Rationalisation had taken place but it had not gone far enough.

The British economy, depending to a substantial extent on overseas trade, had proved particularly vulnerable to circumstances created or stimulated by the war years. Steep tariffs and other forms of government discrimination reduced opportunities in many markets and could lead to dumping in Britain. The world's capacity to produce many goods had been greatly enhanced by the circumstances of war, but in the post-war years the need or ability to purchase or consume had been reduced. Though British industry fared better in the 1930s than in the 1920s, the improvement was based more on home demand than any marked recovery of overseas sales. Moreover, for all the improved aggregate output, indicators of productivity generally showed Britain performing relatively badly throughout the inter-war years. However, it must be pointed out that, in respect of Europe, this was generally in the context of other countries needing to catch up.

Government policy, or lack of it, has sometimes been held accountable for a substantial proportion of Britain's inter-war economic ills. It is certainly true that the state was reluctant to interfere directly in industrial matters, a characteristic of most governments at that time and, in the light of post-war experience, not necessarily a mistaken position. The return to gold in 1925 and associated deflationary policies may have depressed home demand but there is little evidence that it had an adverse effect on overseas trade. In spite of a nominal commitment to free trade, strategic industries, including important high-technology sectors, were protected from 1915 and there was general protection and other forms of intervention in the free market in the 1930s, though the effects even then were uneven [38].

Much has been made of the organisational deficiencies and technical backwardness of older staples. Though there were exceptions, even in cotton and coal-mining, these criticisms were generally well-founded. But they were, in the main, products of the long life of these industries (old mills, old pits, old shipyards), and much capital, let alone skilled labour, was tied up in them. Moreover, with poor trading conditions and small- and large-scale firms heavily in debt or struggling to make any profit at all, the circumstances were hardly conducive to high-cost re-location and re-equipment. Poor or uninspired management may have compounded the problems of some firms and industries but the root cause was generally an external one.

4   1939–1979: LOST OPPORTUNITIES?

The economic effects of the war of 1939–45 were of an altogether different order from those of the war of 1914–18. Unemployment was eliminated, though not until after 1940, and did not re-appear on any scale for over 30 years. Indeed, during the 1940s and for much of the 1950s, the economy was characterised by labour shortage. High lev-els of employment and rising incomes coincided with the need, both at home and abroad, to make good the physical damage of war as well as neglected investment and increased public spending on education and welfare. The result was unprecedented affluence and the apparent conquest of poverty. In such circumstances, weaknesses in Britain's economic condition went largely unremarked before the 1960s.

In general terms, the years 1939–79 saw, first, periods of war and readjustment (1939–45 and 1945–50) in which British economic performance appeared creditable, then a period of economic prosperity (1950s and 1960s, extending until 1973) during which the British economy, by historical standards, did well but other major economies did better, and, finally, a period of economic uncertainty (the middle and late 1970s) when most economies faltered but that of Britain seemed to perform particularly badly.

The Second World War converted Britain from the world's largest creditor nation into its largest debtor and established, temporarily at least, a client relationship with the USA. However, the immediate post-war economy shared many characteristics with the earlier part of the century. Manufacturing employed 45% of the labour force and contributed one-third of the manufactured exports of the world's leading industrial economies. By contrast, less than 20% of imports were in the form of manufactures [24, Millward in 92].

This manufacturing base still rested on traditional staples and the growth industries of the pre-1939 period. In 1950, the UK supplied over 15% of world cotton exports, employing nearly a quarter of a million operatives in spinning and weaving. In the same year, coal output stood at nearly 220 million tons, of which over 17 million were exported. There were 901 National Coal Board pits and the industry employed a workforce of 691,000. The shipbuilding industry was the world's leading producer, launching in excess of 1.3 million gross tons and employing a workforce of 302,000. Steel production, at 16.3 million tons, was 30% above its peak pre-war level [102, 122, Thomas in 23].

Among newer industries, the motor vehicle industry was the world's largest exporter with over half of world exports in 1950, a year in which 75% of all cars produced and more than 60% of commercial vehicles were sold overseas. Imports, to a protected market, were minimal; 'transport equipment and machinery' accounted for just 2.4% of total UK imports in 1951. Total production, from an industry still largely in British hands, stood at 522,000 cars and 261,000 commercial vehicles. Chemical industries, benefiting from the temporary removal of German competition, and the increasing importance of petro-chemicals, also grew strongly with 42% expansion between 1946 and 1950 [*Doc. 16*]. The same period saw, in favourable circumstances, a 34% expansion in the value of chemical exports. Electrical engineering was also performing strongly, with the electronics sector, boosted by demand for radios and televisions, employing 93,000 people by 1950 [47, Millward in 92, 107].

By 1979, although exports of manufactures still narrowly outweighed imports, Britain's standing in the industrial and trading world had diminished substantially and there had been dramatic changes in the industrial base. The cotton industry was, by now, insignificant. Much of what was left was linked to the chemical industries and the manufacture of artificial fibres. Cotton exports, which were minimal, were far outweighed by imports. Though British shipyards – now heavily subsidised – continued during the 1970s to launch an average of more than 1.2 million tons a year, they had failed to share in the 10% a year expansion of world output that had characterised the period 1955–75. As a result, British yards' share of tonnage launched had fallen to between 3% and 5% and the country was ranked eleventh among the world's shipbuilders. Coal output was down to under 120 million tons with just 2.5 million tons exported (the country had become a net coal importer). Employment had fallen to 234,900 and the number of collieries to 223. Steel output, at 21.5 million tons, was a quarter down on the level of 1970 [16, Thomas in 23, 102, 123].

Total motor vehicle production, while one-third down on a 1972 peak, still stood, in 1979, at over 1.2 million, nearly 60% higher than in 1950. However, in several respects the situation resembled that of older staples. Britain's share of world exports had fallen dramatically to 9% of cars and 11% of commercial vehicles by 1974, and continued falling to 2% of both categories by 1986. The country had become a net importer of cars from 1973 and of commercial vehicles from 1977. Moreover, British Leyland, the one volume producer still in British hands, had seen its market share halved in a decade to around 20% [23, Millward in 92, 107].

But although the decline, relative or absolute, of particular industries attracted comment, the issue had become one of the economy as a whole. By 1979, Britain's was seen as the sick economy of Europe. Earlier explanations based on other countries 'catching up' had been abandoned. The term 'de-industrialisation' was in common use. Economic debate turned not only on how the country's current economic condition had come about but on whether it was even possible to reverse it [1, 3].

WAR YEARS, 1939–45

The war of 1939–45 involved mobilisation of the British economy on a far greater scale than that of 1914–18. It also brought to an end the under-utilisation of resources that had characterised the 1920s and 1930s, though this did not happen immediately. Demands of war distorted the economy, giving an enormous stimulation to industries and services essential to the war effort and forcing stagnation or decline on others. A range of industries producing consumer goods for the domestic market contracted. Trade, too, diminished and the deficit on visible items widened significantly. Exports fell by over 70% in volume and halved in value between 1938 and 1943, while imports fell by nearly a quarter in volume though they did rise by a third in value in the same period. This, along with other wartime commitments, undermined a previously healthy balance on the external account [88, Howlett in 92] [*Doc. 14*].

Industries benefiting from the war included shipbuilding where output, though handicapped by shortages of labour, steel and berths, grew to more than 1.8 million tons a year in 1942 and 1943, with merchant vessels making up two-thirds of this figure. In addition, during any one week during the war, shipyards were engaged in the repair of between 700 and 1,000 vessels. The workforce of 145,000 in 1939 rose sharply to 272,000 by late 1943.

In the chemicals industries, within overall expansion there was a marked shift of capacity towards products essential to the war effort.

Numbers employed more than doubled from 294,000 in 1939 to 618,000 in 1942 and remained at more than half a million in 1943 and 1944. There was also substantial commitment to additional capacity, the government investing £58 million in plant managed by ICI alone. Important growth sectors included sulphuric acid (where output increased from 1.1 million tons in 1939 to more than 1.25 million in the years 1942–44), nitrogenous and phosphate fertilisers (up 50% and 60% respectively over the course of the war), and plastics and synthetic resin (where annual production rose by 50% between 1941 and 1943–45). Rayon output, by contrast, was cut back to about half the pre-war figure [47, 116, Vol. 2].

Similarly, in electrical and electronic engineering there was a contrast between sharp cutbacks in civilian production (e.g. output of radios for civilian use was cut from 2 million a year in the late 1930s to 50,000 in 1944) and a stimulus to development and mass production for military purposes. Production of radio valves, for example, trebled from less than 12 million a year in 1939 to more than 35 million in 1944. The electrical engineering workforce also grew substantially with the number of male workers staying constant at 110–120,000 but the number of women workers more than doubling from 79,500 in 1939 to over 180,000 in 1944 [88, 97].

War was also good for farming. Production and consumption of fertilisers doubled during the war years. There was a similar growth in the number of tractors in use and a substantial increase in use of other agricultural equipment. Arable land increased by over 50% during the course of the war, with wheat production more than doubling between 1939 and 1943 and potato output increasing by not much less during the same period.

Machine tool output grew from 37,000 machines in 1939 to a peak of 96,000 in 1942, though it was still necessary to import items like automatic lathes and vertical drillers from the USA. Production of aircraft grew spectacularly in spite of constant changes in specification (nearly 1,100 in the case of the Spitfire alone between 1938 and 1945), ever greater levels of sophistication and, in the case of bombers, larger machines (e.g. a 1944 Lancaster was more than twice the weight of a 1939 Wellington). A three-fold growth to 2,800 over the years 1935–38 was followed by 7,940 in 1939, over 24,000 in 1941 and more than 26,000 in each of the years 1943 and 1944.

The steel industry, while prosperous as a result of the war, did not increase output above the late 1930s peak of just over 12 million tons a year. Here, First World War lessons about the lead times necessary to boost production had been learned. Wartime demand was met by cutting amounts used in the civilian economy and by a marked increase in imports [88, Howlett in 92, 97].

Coal-mining was also vital to the war effort but here Second World War performance was disappointing. Production fell from 231 million tons in 1939 to 183 million by 1945. Over the same period, the workforce and labour productivity also declined, by 57,000 and by 6 cwt (10%) per coalface shift. There were a number of reasons for this, not all of them avoidable. In the circumstances of war, current seams were exploited for quick return and there was little commitment to opening up new resources, hence output declined as seams approached exhaustion. Miners, too, were getting older. By 1942, more than 40% of the workforce were aged over 40 and 20% were over 50. This contributed to absenteeism where the 1945 figure was more than double that of 1939. All this was in the context of rising demand from power stations and gasworks. However, export and bunker shipments were reduced from 46.5 million tons in 1939 to 6.1 million in 1944 and a further 8 million tons of coal were obtained from open cast workings. This kept domestic supplies at or above 1939 levels until 1944 [88, 93, 124].

Cotton was one of the industries subject to a Board of Trade policy whereby restricted production was concentrated in a small number of nucleus establishments, releasing other plant and labour for war work. In spinning and weaving, production was concentrated in 280 mills containing some 24 million spindles, about 60% of the industry total. Weaving production was similarly concentrated. It has been argued that wartime concentration of what was an indispensable industry went too far. On the other hand, labour and raw material shortages meant that even the remaining plant was under-utilised. In 1944, only 72% of nucleus firms' spindles and 80% of their looms were operating. Output of cotton cloth settled at about half that of 1937. Of longer-term significance, war suspended the process of rationalisation and modernisation of the cotton industry as well as contributing to an artificially favourable position in world markets during the late 1940s [93, 96].

Overall, the British economy expanded rapidly in the period 1939–43, falling back thereafter. Real national product rose by 27% between 1939 and 1943 (with the biggest increase between 1939 and 1940) and per capita GDP grew by 14% per person employed. Only the US economy, with a 49% increase in national product over the same period, performed better. By contrast, Germany experienced only a 16% increase and the USSR, where invasion led to considerable loss of territory, saw a decline of 34%. The increase in real income represented more than half the domestic resources needed for combat purposes.

These figures hide substantial changes in patterns of income and expenditure. Personal expenditure on goods and services grew from £4,422 million in 1939 to £5,291 million in 1943; public expenditure (increasingly war-related) grew from £1,198 to £5,054 million in the same period. This period also saw negative non-war capital formation and net overseas disinvestment [*Doc. 13*] which, together with financial claims from overseas, averaged £642.6 million a year [88, Howlett in 92, 94].

The UK has been presented as the most successful combatant power in terms of mobilisation for the Second World War. Figures, however, suggest that this claim has to be treated with caution. German output and productivity in important areas including machine tools and armoured fighting vehicles was greater. In terms of domestic finance committed to war purposes, the UK peak of 47% in 1943 and 1944 is lower than the USA's peak of 54%, the USSR's 66% and Germany's 60% (all 1944). Britain did make more use of overseas resources (including lend-lease* and overseas investment incomes), but, even when these are taken into account, the proportion of national income devoted to war purposes was less than that of Germany or the USSR [85, 94].

However, to sustain over time the scale of military effort demanded in the Second World War required an appropriate balance in the allocation of personnel between the fighting forces, production of war supplies and the maintenance of civilian goods and services. Here, British mobilisation proved very successful. By 1943, 45.3% of the workforce was divided, more or less evenly, between the armed forces and war-related industry. The remainder, just over half, provided for civilian needs. Of the other major combatant nations, the USSR had 54% mobilised for war purposes, the USA 35.4% and Germany, where numbers in the armed forces outnumbered those in war industry by more than three to two, 37.6%. In terms of efficient overall use of labour, the USA performed best and Germany worst.

Over the whole period of the war, imports of resources, obtained principally through lend-lease, were more important to Britain than to any other power. It has been calculated that they totalled more than a year's pre-war national income. By 1944, over 40% of armaments came from overseas [94].

Much of the above information is itself a consequence of a wartime development of lasting economic significance. In a bid to meet the demands of war and, at the same time, curb powerful inflationary pressures, budgets from 1941 onwards utilised estimates of national income and elements of Keynesian economic theory in taking, for the state, a much more pro-active economic role than had been known hitherto. Economic management became the major purpose of budgetary policy [88].

Analysis of the economic impact of war involves more, then, than consideration of sectors that grew and sectors that were curtailed during the period of military activity. It demands, as we have seen, a comparison of Britain's economic achievements in relation to the war with those of other combatant powers. It includes, too, assessment of whether war advanced or hindered longer-term prospects. Did war contribute to lasting changes in the goods produced by British industry? Did wartime stress on production rather than productivity or the distorted investment of the period reduce growth potential? Did the removal of Japan or Germany as rivals in world markets offset the advantages seized by the USA as a result of the war? Was Britain's relative performance post-war enhanced or held back by the lack of destruction of plant, equipment or economic institutions when compared to the experience in Japan or much of western Europe? To what extent did wartime experience lead to a more constructive economic role for government? Answers to these questions will, of course, only become apparent as we study the post-war period.

RECONSTRUCTION, 1945–50

The post-war world presented opportunity, restraint and potential threats to Britain's economic wellbeing. In the short term, major rivals like Germany and Japan were eliminated at a time when the world was crying out for consumer and capital goods in short supply during the war years. At home, too, full employment, increased real incomes and accumulated savings created buoyant demand. The commitment of governments, at home and abroad, to managing their countries' economies, whatever the practical limitations to such policies, contributed to a climate of economic confidence. Greatly increased welfare spending, maligned by some as a diversion of economic resources from more rewarding activity, not only maintained the spending power of poorer members of the community but, in a host of ways, generated demand for buildings, equipment, drugs and other consumables, as well as creating an enlarged professional middle class with economic demands of its own [84, 85, 95].

To set against these opportunities, there were short-term restraints and longer-term potential threats. Immediate constraints included the disruption and impoverishment of traditional European markets in the immediate post-war years and shortages of labour, equipment and raw materials. Raw material and equipment problems were compounded by Britain's lack of dollars.

The demands of the post-war years saw continued emphasis on production rather than productivity, although, taking the economy as a whole, the latter did improve by some 20% between 1938 and 1950. Manufacturers continued to use existing plant and equipment, most of which had survived the war intact. An acute labour shortage contributed to the restoration of traditional working practices. Indeed, the post-war economic climate, like the war itself, served to hinder processes of modernisation and rationalisation that had been forced upon employers and labour in the more difficult conditions of the 1920s and 1930s.

In examining post-war performance, the first task is to evaluate management of the transition to peace and Britain's economic achievement by the early 1950s. By 1951, GDP stood 22% higher than in 1938, compared to 5% higher in 1946. This overall figure masked significant contrasts by sector. The utilities (gas, water and electricity) had increased by 83%, manufacturing by 43%, insurance, banking and finance by 13%. Public administration and defence, which had increased by 140% during the period 1938–46, had been pegged back to a 52% increase by 1952. By contrast, mining and quarrying was still 9% below the 1938 figure and building and construction 12% [84, Leyland in 100].

Post-war economic growth was led by exports. Overseas sales quadrupled between 1945 and 1951 and the UK's share of world exports increased from 17.5% in the immediate pre-war period to 20.7% in 1950. This was in part a consequence of government policy, an export drive which, coupled with curbs on imports, aimed to restore equilibrium in the current trading account and, in particular, to reduce the so-called 'dollar gap'*. Much more, however, it reflected a sellers' market and a surge in world manufactured exports to a level, by 1950, 21% above that of pre-war, with European exports as a whole growing faster than those of the UK after 1948. Moreover, much of Britain's trade was with the sterling area, where competition was limited, rather than wealthier North American or western European markets. Indeed, by 1951, over half UK exports were to that area compared to 45% in 1938. More encouragingly, two-thirds of exports, by the early 1950s, were in products where world trade was expanding: chemicals (including artificial fibres), motor vehicles, petroleum products, pharmaceuticals.

Overall, however, in spite of periodic crises and warning signals for the future, the British economy was, by 1950, in a sound condition. The problem of the dollar gap had been much diminished, although, taking up one of the questions posed at the end of the previous section, the competitive situation of the USA had been greatly strengthened. The difficult process of adjustment after the greatest and most destructive war in history had been managed, though not without help from the USA. Government did accept a more positive role in economic management in spite of the fact that the statistical tools at its disposal remained primitive. The strength of the economy in areas of growing world trade suggested that the effect of wartime patterns of investment had been broadly positive. Overall, in the late 1940s there had been a clear sense of policy and direction [24, 86].

LOSING GROUND, THE 1950s AND 1960s

Between 1951 and 1973, GDP grew at an average of 2.8% a year. Historically, this was a strong performance, better than the 2.2% a year achieved between 1856 and 1873 (the 'great Victorian boom') or again between 1924 and 1937, or the 1.8% a year of the period 1937–51. Other indicators give a similarly encouraging picture: between 1950 and 1973, GDP per person hour grew at an annual rate of 3.2%; the volume of UK exports grew by 143% between 1950 and 1975. Invisible trade was once more in credit by 1948 and outweighed the deficit on the visible balance in most years until 1973, though the mid-1960s saw an exception to this. And yet, this was the period when British decline became the accepted and unchallenged economic and political wisdom [41, 42, 99].

The explanation lies in the comparative performance of the British and other economies and the painful realisation, over time, that this was not just a case of other countries coming closer to Britain in absolute levels of economic achievement but one in which Britain was eventually overtaken. In terms of GDP per head, only the USA, Switzerland, Canada and Australia in the developed world outperformed the UK in 1950. By 1973, though there had been a marginal improvement in the British position compared to that of the USA, the UK had been caught by Germany and overtaken by France, Denmark, the Netherlands and Sweden and the gap between Britain and other states was narrowing rapidly. In terms of GDP per hour worked, in 1950 workers in the USA produced 185% of the figure for those in the UK, but workers in France, Germany and Japan, only 70%, 54%

and 24% respectively. By 1973, the gap between the American and UK figures had been reduced to 56% but the French had overtaken the UK and the Germans had caught up. The Japanese figure still stood at only 62%, a reminder of the great gap in productivity between the export-led and other sectors of the Japanese economy. Britain's share of world exports of manufactures fell meantime from 25.5% in 1950 (second only to the USA with 27.3%) to 9.3% in 1975 when she came fifth behind the German Federal Republic (20.3%), USA (17.7%), Japan (13.6%) and France (10.2%) [41, 84, Crafts in 89].

Emphasis on relative decline has led, in recent times, to some neglect of the question of why the British, like other economies, grew so strongly and consistently, with trade cycle fluctuations much reduced, during the quarter-century or so after the war. Keynesian economic management has been discounted, at least in terms of its direct effects. Government fiscal policy during this period was generally deflationary and has even been portrayed as destabilising, exaggerating such fluctuations as did occur. More important was the enormous pent-up demand for capital and consumer goods following a lengthy and destructive war involving all the world's major industrial powers, creating an international secular boom which fed on itself. The continuation of this boom was assisted by the different timing of downturns that did occur in different countries. It was further sustained by increased government spending, here and abroad, on welfare and on maintaining military power, and possibly by the very confidence, misguided or otherwise, generated by political commitment to high levels of employment and demand [84, 90, 95].

Why did the economies of other countries perform so much better than that of Britain? During the 1950s and 1960s, much of this gain did take the form of convergence. As we have seen, Britain started with a high level of GDP per capita, one which only fell below that of the Organisation for Economic Co-operation and Development (OECD)*, as a whole, in the late 1960s. In the 1950s, moreover, a number of other countries were still recovering from the devastation of war and gained, too, from the ability to transfer labour from low-productivity agriculture into higher-productivity manufacturing industry or services. Indeed this, and Britain's relatively low rate of population growth, has been seen as accounting for half the growth differential between Britain and other European states during the 1950s. Later developing economies, moreover, had less capital and less organisational commitment to existing processes. This made for lower cost of, and resistance to, innovation, and they were able also to take advantage of lessons to be learned from more advanced economies such as that of the UK [41, 43].

A number of analysts in the 1960s and 1970s saw the role of government as unhelpful to the national economic cause. A particularly interesting contribution was that of W.A.P. Manser. Manser had resigned as Head of Public Relations at the British Iron and Steel Federation when the Labour government re-nationalised it in 1967, and he subsequently found work with Barings Bank. While this background should be borne in mind, it does not undermine the core of his argument. Manser pointed out that not only had there always been a visible trade gap, but that this gap, as a percentage of imports, had been smaller after 1945 than in preceding years. Invisibles had, of course, normally been sufficient to provide an overall surplus in the balance of payments. Even after the disinvestment of the Second World War, they had been sufficient to create a net balance over the years 1946–63. Only in the period 1964–68 had there been the abnormality of substantial net deficits; thus there was not a long-term balance of payments crisis. Insofar as the invisibles balance, post-war, had been less positive than in earlier times, this was the result of deficits on the government account. As an item, these had been self-balancing until the 1930s and they had only become a serious negative item in the post-war period. Essentially, they were caused by the probably unavoidable military cost of trying to play a world-wide role. The USA, but no other state, carried a similar burden. Were Germany and Japan to carry negative public external balances on the scale of Britain, their overall balances of payments would be pushed into deficit [14, 18].

For Manser, governments, having caused the problem, then compounded it. Public statements drew attention to balance of payments difficulties and contributed to short-term outflows of money. In a bid to shore up the pound, they kept the economy almost permanently deflated (a point also made by Matthews); this had been the cause of Britain's slow growth. Britain could solve its 'problems' by going for growth [14].

Manser was also concerned by what Americans would call 'big government', the mounting sums (£15 billion by 1968) 'siphoned off' from the private sector. In this, he anticipated the so-called Bacon and Eltis thesis: the tendency for governments in developed countries to spend increasing amounts on non-market goods, mostly in the field of welfare. This, it was held, drew off labour, forcing industry to contract. Moreover, the high taxation needed to sustain such spending reduced profits and savings as sources of investment and, since workers resisted any reduction in consumption standards, demands for higher money wages fuelled inflation or further reduced company profits. The thesis, however, was open to a number of criticisms. There was no evidence of British manufacturing industry suffering from a shortage of finance or of labour in the 1960s and early 1970s. A particular weakness, from this point of view, was the fact that whereas 72% of the fall in the industrial workforce (1966–76) was male, 74% of increased employment in the 'non market' sector was female. Nor, in other developed countries like West Germany, had the growth of the government sector been accompanied by a fall in the industrial labour force. Indeed, for Britain, increased employment in services generally, including those provided by central and local government, had kept unemployment lower than it would otherwise have been [2, Thatcher, Stout in 3, 22].

Nor was industry heavily taxed. Studies suggest that the burden of corporate taxation was low and generally declining from the 1950s to the 1970s. The regime in the 1970s was to be even more generous, particularly in respect of depreciation allowances. One commentator, implying a regime so generous as to be demotivating, has gone so far as to call it 'a vast and undiscriminating system of outdoor relief for British manufacturers' [23].

Further criticisms of government, both in the 1960s and a decade later, drew attention to the supposed effects of 'stop–go' policies, the contradictions inherent in the plurality of government economic objectives, lack of policy at the operational or firm level by contrast with contemporary economic fast-movers like France or Japan, the failure to maximise development in the nationalised industries, and, above all, the lack of political will. So-called 'stop–go' involved an alternating pattern of expansionist and retrenchment policies as government tried to maintain growth and employment but without creating inflation, strains on the balance of payments and a short-term run on sterling holdings. It was held to create business uncertainty and thus hinder growth. In fact, the resulting economic fluctuations of the 1950s and 1960s were mild by the standards of what preceded and succeeded them and the experiences were shared by most developed economies, including those with more impressive growth records than the UK [16, 23, 25].

A similar defence of British governments can be made in respect of the demands made by competing policies. Thus pursuit of competition or full employment and regional development could conflict with a quest for rationalisation of industry. General Electric Company

(GEC) was a government-supported rationalisation of the electrical engineering industry, but it was achieved at the expense of competition and jobs. A similar tension was apparent between the needs of the regions and rational development of British car manufacture during the 1960s and 1970s. But this was an inevitable problem of government intervention in any complex developed economy [23].

There is a little more substance to the suggestion that the long-term potential of nationalised industries was subordinated to short-term political or economic objectives or that economic planning failed at an operational level. The mismanagement of the nationalised sector has been well chronicled. Investment and pricing policy in the original nationalised utilities fell victim to the demands of macro-economic policy in the 1950s, with secondary consequences for supplying industries, e.g. manufacturers of heavy electrical generating equipment. Later nationalisations in the 1970s were of ailing industries threatened with collapse. Government policy, in this context, was essentially one of ensuring survival rather than establishing a long-term strategy. The introduction of the semi-independent National Enterprise Board (NEB), in 1976, to hold shares in British Leyland and Rolls Royce, was a potentially significant innovation. However, the anti-interventionist economic ideology of the Conservative government elected in 1979 and the slump of 1979–81 gave the NEB little opportunity to be effective.

Nor, in the economy at large, was there British intervention equivalent to that of the Japanese Ministry of International Trade and Industry (MITI)* or the French government with its plans and national 'champions' in major sectors. The National Economic Development Council* and its sector working parties, the 'little Neddies', failed to plan below the industry level. There was no attempt to, or means of, operationalising these plans by tying targets to individual enterprises. However, it should be pointed out that the Japanese and French strategies were very different from one another and the national circumstances of those countries bore little resemblance to those of Britain. Moreover, other countries without such positive government intervention also out-performed the UK. Greater intervention, alone, would not have solved Britain's apparent problems [23, 25].

CRISIS MANAGEMENT, THE 1970s

The 1970s marked the end of the general prosperity, and relative economic stability, of the post-war period. In Britain, it was a decade characterised by unemployment on a scale unknown since before the

war, by inflation unmatched since the First World War and im
ately after, by the biggest setback in output since the beginning or the
1930s, by horrendous deficit on the current account, by industrial un-
rest and by crises in particular industries and firms that drove Labour
and Conservative governments alike to take ailing enterprises into
public ownership. All this was in the context of a new relationship
with Europe within the European Economic Community (EEC)*,
wild fluctuations in the value of a currency allowed to float from
1972 and, at the end of the decade, the availability of North Sea oil.

At the beginning of the decade, the economic signals for Britain
were mixed. 1973 was the peak of a spectacular boom, a year in
which output grew by 7.3%, more than in any other post-war year.
International economic expansion was reinforced, in the UK, by the
1971 removal of curbs on bank credits and sharp and inflationary increases in bank lending, by 37% in 1972 and 43% in 1973. Against
this, annual inflation levels, well below 5% since the early 1950s, had
crossed that boundary in 1969 and continued to rise, averaging 8.8%
over the years 1971–73. The period was also characterised by major
industrial disputes, notably in the coal-mining industry, and by government intervention to take over or bale out particular firms or
industries in danger of collapse, including Rolls Royce (1971) and the
shipbuilding industry [87].

At the end of 1973, in the wake of the newly formed cartel, the Organisation of Petroleum Exporting Countries (OPEC)*, oil prices
quadrupled. This huge economic shock had a dramatic impact on industrialised economies accustomed to cheap fuel. The effect was
compounded by the effects of the oil price increase on other supplies,
food and the products of extractive industries. The result for the UK
was an increase in import prices of 55% in the year to the first quarter of 1974, retail price increases that peaked in August 1975 at an
annual rate of 27%, a record deficit of £3.2 billion on the current account for 1974, and a sharp downturn in economic activity with
GDP falling by 3.9% in 1974 and 2.1% in 1975. These conditions,
taken alongside other perceived weaknesses in the British economy,
led to loss of confidence in sterling. The pound, allowed to float from
its 1968 parity of $2.40 from 1972, was trading at $1.55 by October
1976 [87].

The impact of increased oil prices was severe but temporary. By
contrast with the slump of the 1930s, primary producers were not im-
poverished, indeed the OPEC countries had to recycle their vast
dollar incomes. In addition, the industrialised world now recognised
its economic interdependency and had, through the US-dominated In-

ternational Monetary Fund (IMF)*, a means of organising a co-
ordinated response. It was also a world accustomed to economic
innovation and technological change; fuel economy was to be a
marked feature of the response to changed circumstances. A further
factor, in the longer term, was that these changed circumstances had
been the work of a cartel which would have to hold together if the
new pricing alignments were to survive [25].

The British economy continued to perform relatively badly. Inflation, though falling from the mid-1970s peak, remained generally in
double figures, averaging 16% for the period 1973–79 compared to
9% for the OECD as a whole. Average annual growth of per capita
GDP for the years 1973–79 was 1.5%, compared to 2.9% for 1968–
73. Among major economies, only the USA, averaging 1.4% (compared
to 1.8% 1968–73), fared worse. However, with Italy, Japan, Germany and France achieving 1973–79 averages of between 2.1% and
2.6% (compared to 3.9% to 6.8% for the preceding period), there
was a significant narrowing of the differential between British performance and that of competitors [25, Supple in 92] [*Doc. 20*].

By 1979, supplies of North Sea oil were beginning to build up,
helping reduce Britain's import dependency. The mid-1970s slump
and the urgent quest for fuel economy had already combined, in
probably equal measure, to reduce imports. This reinforced a trend,
apparent since the mid-1960s. Traditional industries such as textile or
iron and steel manufacture and shipbuilding, using imports of raw
cotton, wool, iron ore, jute, wood or rubber, were in decline. They
were being replaced by products using solid state technology or synthetic materials based on oil or gas. Increased self-sufficiency in
foodstuffs, another longer-term trend, proved a further important
brake on imports, though the increase over the decade was, in value
terms, the largest on record.

Import growth was, however, outweighed by that of exports.
These, aided later in the decade by oil sales, increased in value and
volume by more than imports, in the latter case for the first time since
the immediate post-war years. This trade was, more than ever, centred on western Europe. Britain had joined the EEC in 1973 but
growing inter-dependency with this area had been a characteristic
since at least the early 1960s. In 1958, the 'Old Commonwealth'
('White Dominions') and less developed economies (many in the so-
called 'New Commonwealth') had taken some 46% of British exports
compared to western Europe's 30%. By 1965 the figures were 34.5%
and 41.7% respectively. In 1973 and 1979, western Europe took
56.8% and 58.2% of British exports and the 'Old Commonwealth'/

less developed economies 21.4% and 15.7%. The proportion of trade with the USA had also risen slightly since the late 1950s. Thus Britain was trading to an increasing extent with the wealthier, developed economies of the world [25, 87].

Longer-term failure to achieve an export growth which matched that of imports was one widely favoured explanation offered for de-industrialisation by the 1970s. The argument can be considered at two levels. The theoretical position was that a country's economy could only, in the long term, grow at a pace consistent with a balance of payments equilibrium on the current account. Prolonged deficit led to dampening of demand, output unable to grow as fast as productivity and, consequently, mounting unemployment. The practical position, for Britain, was that most manufacturing sectors were facing increasing penetration of their home markets. During the 1970s, the ratio of imports to gross output more than doubled in electrical goods, textiles and clothing and footwear; in motor vehicles it quadrupled. Though, reflecting growing national specialisation of production, ratios of exports to output had also increased, the gains were smaller.

There were, however, two problems with these explanations of relative British performance. First, in the wake of the oil price increases of the mid-1970s, most developed countries were forced to run substantial deficits on the current account. Secondly, and more important, while increased imports and relatively slower export growth could explain much of the loss of employment in manufacturing industry, they remained a symptom of a problem rather than the cause. There was still the question of why the people of the UK were more enthusiastic for imported manufactures than people overseas were for its exports [Singh in 3, 22, 23] [*Doc. 21*].

Why did Britain's manufactured exports continue to grow less rapidly than those of other developed nations and to be outweighed by imports? Lack of price competitiveness does not seem to have been the problem. Although wage costs rose five-fold in Britain between 1963 and 1980, the devaluation and depreciation of sterling meant that this had little effect on the price of goods to overseas buyers. Indeed, the cheapness of many British exports could be seen as a source of weakness; British firms sold too much at the bottom, and less profitable, end of the market. For example, in 1975, West German mechanical engineering exports were worth 60% more per ton than those of Britain.

Nor, in spite of contemporary popular opinion, was any deficient overall performance the result of poor industrial relations, at least insofar as production loss through strikes was concerned. Over the period 1967–76, the UK came near the middle of a table of developed nations in terms of days per thousand workers lost to strikes. Official statistics for the years 1971–75 showed an annual average of 97% of establishments, covering 80% of manufacturing employees, losing no days to strikes [14, 23].

Where there might have been cause for concern was in management of the workplace. Assembly lines were generally over-manned, with British unions, unlike those of, say, the German Federal Republic, able to negotiate unnecessary use of skilled operatives as the price of accepting new technologies. This reduced the productivity gains from innovation and made investment less attractive. Moreover, much machinery was run at less than optimum speed and at lower speeds than in other countries. This has to be set against the apparently reasonable record in industrial relations; 'soft' management might be said to have bought industrial peace. There were many instances where machinery was badly used in other ways. The British car industry, in particular, was notorious for the poor maintenance of equipment leading to breakdowns which added to already over-frequent stoppages in production lines [23, Crafts in 89].

While there was clearly room for improvement in the production process, evidence from the car industry in the 1970s suggests that greater problems lay in marketing. Poor labour productivity, set against lower British wages, added around £25 to the cost of a car built in Britain when compared to one built elsewhere in western Europe. However, model runs that were only half those of continental rivals added, by one calculation, £90 to the development costs of each car. Labour costs could influence the sourcing policies of multinationals like Ford or General Motors (Vauxhall), but for the British producer like British Leyland, the problem of low sales was far more serious.

British Leyland (BLMH), and the British Motor Corporation (BMC) before that, had concentrated on home markets when building up output from 300,000 vehicles a year in the early 1950s to over a million by the mid-1960s. As the British market matured in the 1970s, and replacement demand became all-important, the company (needing to defend a market share of some 40%) found itself assailed by well-equipped continental and Japanese imports which were taking 45% of British private sales by the mid-1970s. Moreover, government taxation policies and pay restraint had led to the company car taking 40% of the overall British market, and Ford, with a better range of larger models, had taken the bulk of this.

Abroad, sales to the USA had been severely affected by the introduction of compact models by American manufacturers at the beginning of the 1960s, while in Europe, where British Leyland cars were assembled in Belgium, Italy and Spain, sales suffered as a result of a poor dealer network and the lack of proper model range (two-thirds of European sales were minis). There was never a network in France or Germany, with the result that, in 1975, British Leyland supplied just over 7,000 of the 3.5 million cars sold in those countries. By 1980, total European sales stood at just 80,000 [11, 23] [*Doc. 19*].

To an extent, the problems of the British car industry abroad were the result of constraints imposed by domestic conditions. Historically, home market conditions have been important for all trade. Only rarely (e.g. in the case of Lancashire cotton) had industries been truly export-led. In the case of British Leyland, a low-wage economy, with the tax-subsidised company market for medium and larger-size cars sewn up by the American Ford company, led to an emphasis on smaller cars that limited the ability to compete in world markets.

Shipbuilding presented a similar case. In the 1950s and 1960s, British builders concentrated on the home market, largely replacing vessels in fleets that were not themselves expanding, on a one-off basis. Flexibility rather than specialism was seen as a form of insurance. Investment in yards fell after the late 1950s, leading to technological backwardness. Thus, when British shipowners took orders abroad in the 1970s, the yards were faced with disaster. Government had to intervene, offering financial inducements to attract business while the yards were reorganised and, in some cases, modernised [23].

BANKS AND INVESTMENT

The role of the banks in relation to industry remained a source of controversy. The 1931 Macmillan Report, suggesting that medium-sized companies were not adequately provided for in capital markets, had been followed by the establishment of institutions like Charterhouse Industrial Development Company, Credit for Industry and Leadenhall Securities Incorporation. The post-war period saw the establishment, by the Bank of England and the major English and Scottish banks, of the Industrial and Commercial Finance Corporation (ICFC), mainly aimed at large firms, and its sister Finance Corporation for Industry (FCI), concentrating on loans to small firms. By the mid-1970s, the latter was lending about £25 million a year and could be described as having been modestly successful. From 1973, the ICFC and FCI were part of Finance for Industry and the resources of that institution were boosted by £1 billion in 1974 in order to provide more medium-term lending (7–15 years). The mid-1970s also saw the British Insurance Association establish Equity Capital for Industry which was aimed at attracting smaller companies [26]. The need for these developments suggests that the banks were not meeting the demands of industry. Certainly, retained profits remained the major source of investment funds, always providing more than 60% in the post-war period. Banks, playing a much smaller role than in Germany or Japan, provided about half of the remainder. Moreover, the banks provided mainly short-term rather than medium- to long-term resources (though loans were often rolled over) and judged creditworthiness on the basis of assets at liquidation rather than, as abroad, on a firm's ability as a going concern to generate funds for repayment. This approach penalised the growing, but still small, as opposed to the established large company. British banks also tended to require small businesses to put up at least matching development funds; in Europe the norm was 20–30%.

In the early post-war period, bank lending was, to a large extent, constrained by government or Bank of England regulation. Moreover, profits at more than 10% were sufficient to provide finance for expansion. However, as profits were squeezed to under 5% between 1974 and 1979, alternative sources of investment became necessary.

Three major reports of the period, those of Radcliffe (1959), Bolton (1971) and Wilson (1980), were broadly supportive of the banks' role, suggesting that the availability and cost of loans in Britain was comparable with the situation overseas. An easing of restrictions in the 1970s, along with an increase in banks' medium-term liabilities, led to a greater readiness to lend over the medium term, though there has been some suggestion that too large a proportion of this increase went into property speculation. The financing of small firms remained, however, a source of difficulty [23, 26] [*Doc. 22*].

And this may have had some influence on the structure of British industry. Although small businesses were not especially vulnerable to failure, their numbers were declining in the late 1950s and early 1960s at a rate of a thousand a year. By the late 1970s, only 29% of British businesses employed under 200 people. The proportion was similar in Germany but much larger, between 40% and 60%, in other developed countries. By comparison, the proportion of giant companies in Britain was growing. The hundred largest firms had been responsible for 22% of output in 1949; this had grown to 41% by the early 1970s (the figure for the USA was a steady 30% or so). This growth was largely by acquisition. The workings of the stock market made takeovers cheap and government was generally acquiescent. However, the profitability record of merged firms was unimpressive. Merger was rarely, as with GEC, followed by rationalisation and firms often failed to solve the more complex managerial problems that accompanied larger companies [23].

RESEARCH AND DEVELOPMENT

Although the exact linkage between research and development (R&D) and economic and trade growth is difficult to pin down, the commonsense view that there is a positive relationship is supported by strong circumstantial evidence. For much of this period, however, Britain's investment in R&D was substantial, though other countries were, in the 1950s and 1960s, gaining and, in the 1970s, overtaking her. Thus, measured in 1985 US dollars, the UK invested $343 per head in 1960, compared to the $803 of the USA, $179 of Germany, $207 of France and just $89 of Japan. By 1973, however, while the USA had maintained its level with $814 and the UK had increased its level to $480, other major economies had increased their R&D levels much more: Germany to $475, France to $448 and Japan to $342 [Freeman in 3, 41].

Even so, given a two to five year lag between investment and trade performance, the figures might have suggested a stronger relative trade performance on the part of Britain, especially during the 1960s. In fact, though, UK R&D was heavily committed to limited areas: 35% of 1962 investment was in the aircraft industry, a figure only exceeded in the USA; 50% of all investment was by government and half of this was in defence-related work in military technology and aerospace. Japan, Germany, France and other European competitors were devoting a greater proportion of their R&D investment to chemicals or electrical and other machinery and instruments. The USA came closest to Britain in patterns of R&D but the sheer scale of that country's investment in areas like aerospace and computers made competition particularly difficult. Moreover, the USA's relatively smaller commitment in sectors such as chemicals and machinery meant that it too was challenged in world markets by Japan and the continental European powers.

British over-commitment of scarce human and capital resources, scientists and engineers, as well as money, to activities where there was little chance of competing with the USA was doubly damaging. Commercial considerations were ignored in 'big technology' projects like Concorde, while mechanical engineering, shipbuilding and other areas of steel and metal goods production were starved in comparison to Germany or Japan. By the end of the 1970s, both those countries annually took out twice the number of US patents that British firms did (Freeman in 3).

CONCLUSION

So, how are we to evaluate economic performance in the 1970s? Certainly, this was a decade of sharp fluctuations in experience and one in which all developed nations had to face new problems. Over the decade there was little increase in fixed capital investment and there was sharp disinvestment in 1974–75. The setback of these years had had no post-war equal. Unemployment, which had re-appeared in Britain in the late 1960s, became a permanent feature of the period, remaining above 3% (historically high by post-war standards) for most of the decade and standing at 4.7% in 1979. Sharp external shocks, notably the international effect of the oil price rise of late 1973, coincided with the problems of particular British industries and firms to create, from time to time, an aura of economic crisis. Problems of industrial relations, not helped by structural and cyclical unemployment running, contrary to Keynesian economic orthodoxy, alongside inflation, came to be seen as a peculiarly British disease, although there was plenty of evidence that it was not. Much of the economic history of the decade has passed into folklore: bailing out 'lame ducks', inflationary pay policies, the miners' overtime ban of 1974 and the three-day week, inflation of 20% or more, Healey* and the IMF, the 'winter of discontent' 1978–79, 'Labour isn't working'. Certainly, this was a decade in which politics was dominated by economic matters, though there is the danger of falling into the usual historians' trap of forcing together widely spaced events – three months (though, unlike politics, perhaps not a week) is a long time in economics. In fact, many of the problems of the 1970s, including slump, 'de-industrialisation', unemployment and inflation, were to re-appear, in much more dramatic form, in the 1980s and 1990s. It is also significant that Britain's 1970s problems were not unique. Indeed the decade could be seen as marking an important turning point. Until the mid-1970s, other economies (certainly in western Europe) had appeared immune to the difficulties facing that of the UK. In the later 1970s, they shared Britain's problems, even if (on the whole) they still coped better.

Be that as it may, by the end of the decade, concern at what was conceived as a peculiarly British problem led to real pessimism as to whether a democratic government, ruling by consent, could take the actions necessary to turn the economy round.

5 FROM THE ASHES? THE BRITISH ECONOMY SINCE 1979

The 1970s had seen the end of post-war optimism that cyclical decline and mass unemployment had been defeated. The 1980s and 1990s were to produce world and British economic experiences that appeared to have much in common with the inter-war years. Deep cyclical slumps at the beginning of each decade were followed by prolonged periods of recovery. Though many additional jobs were created, structural adjustments, first in manufacturing industry and later in service sectors, contributed to levels of unemployment not known since the 1920s and 1930s. This rapidly changing economy created new standards of material wellbeing for many but a significant minority were excluded from its benefits. Society's divisions became much more apparent. While the relative performance of the British economy remained open to debate, for much of the period it was no longer the case that the country was doing significantly worse than others and Conservative politicians were able to claim (with some support from statistics) that Britain was actually out-performing many of her economic rivals.

THE 1980s

The slump of 1979–82 was deep and sharp. GDP at factor cost fell by £6.0 billion between 1979 and 1981 and by a further £3.2 billion between 1981 and 1982. The 14.5% fall in manufacturing output was steeper than that of 1929–31. Company liquidations reached a record figure of 12,000 in 1982. Employment in manufacturing fell by 24% between 1979 and 1983, and unemployment, which had stood at 1 million in 1979, doubled to more than 2 million by 1981 and went on to reach well over 3 million by 1983. The slump followed a second sharp increase in world oil prices, one from which Britain, with North Sea oil now well on stream, might have been expected to benefit.

In fact, North Sea oil contributed £6 billion net in 1980 and £9 billion in 1981. Sterling's attraction as a petro-currency contributed to the pound rising from $2.15 in October 1979 to $2.42 a year later. This could, of course, have made exports of manufactures difficult, but, in fact, they remained unchanged during 1979–80 and only fell 4% between 1980 and 1983. Nor could the problems of manufacturing be put down to dramatically increased imports. Manufactured imports fell between 1979 and 1981, though they did recover sharply, reaching a level 17% above that of 1979 by 1983, taking Britain into deficit in this aspect of the external account. The major cause of falling GDP and rising unemployment appears, rather, to have been very tight monetary policy. Bank rate stood at 14% or over for nearly two years beginning in the summer of 1979 and was at that level again during the winter of 1981–82. Businesses ran down stocks over the whole period 1980–82. Margaret Thatcher's Conservative regime was committed to reducing the role and cost of government. In spite of increased demands on the social security budget, increases in government expenditure were much lower than in previous decades [25, 37, 87].

Britain's economic experience, 1979–82, was worse than that of other industrial economies. The fall in GDP came earlier and was steeper than elsewhere. Overall, the GDPs of OECD countries rose by 1–1½% p.a. in the years 1979–81 and fell only marginally (at a time when Britain had turned the corner) between 1981 and 1982. British unemployment, meantime, rose from 5% in 1979 to 12.4% in 1983. The OECD average, over the same period, increased at a more modest rate, from 5% to 8.5% [41, 87].

As 50 years earlier, deep slump was followed by an economic growth that was sustained for the remainder of the 1980s. As in the 1930s, this growth, which created dramatic increases in real incomes for the majority of the population, failed to eliminate the problem of unemployment. In a further similarity with the 1930s, British economic performance began to compare favourably with that of other countries. Growth averaging 3.6% a year in the five years to 1987–88, while less than that of Japan (4.5%) or the USA (4.4%), was comfortably ahead of the rates of 2.5% in Germany, 2.2% in France or 3.0% in Italy. Much of this was making up for the unusually bad experience at the beginning of the decade. However, over the decade 1979–89, UK GDP growth of 26.8%, while low by 1950s or 1960s standards, was marginally greater than the figure of 24.3% for the EEC as a whole. This represented a sharp contrast with consistently inferior relative performance during the preceding three decades [43] [Doc. 27].

What were the characteristics of the 1980s economy? A major feature was the shake-out of labour from declining and successful industries alike. The decade saw shipbuilding and coal-mining reduced to the status of minor industries in terms of goods produced and numbers employed. It saw a continued relative decline in the British car industry and the numbers employed in it. Here the 450,000 jobs which had survived in spite of the industry's problems during the 1970s were reduced to 290,000 by 1983, with British Leyland alone shedding 53% of its workforce in the six years to 1983. The sourcing policies of multi-nationals like Ford and General Motors make it difficult to estimate accurately the extent of this decline. However, British Leyland's output of cars, while recovering in the late 1980s, averaged just 435,000 a year, 60% of the figure for the 1970s. The company's UK market share, once 40% and still close to 20% at the end of the 1970s, fell to under 15%.

The decade also saw a sharp reduction in plant operated and numbers employed in more successful industries. In steel, employment fell by 61% between 1977 and 1983, while output shrank to about two-thirds its late 1970s level before climbing to nearer 90% of that figure in the late 1980s boom. Chemicals and the media were other examples of prosperous industries which also shed labour on a large scale.

Overall, manufacturing declined sharply in relative importance. The sector had provided 28% of GDP in 1972; this fell to 21% by 1983. It was 1988 before output recovered to 1979 levels. A consequence of this process, as domestic consumption of manufactures rose by nearly a third, 1979–89, sucking in imports, was that the traditional trade surplus in manufactured goods had become a £16.1 billion deficit (3.1% of GDP) by 1989 [7, 12, 37].

Falling employment in the early 1980s was accompanied by more flexible working practices. Numbers employed in manufacturing, which had stood at some 9 million and nearly 40% of the labour force in the mid-1960s, had fallen to around 7 million (32%) in 1980 and continued to decline to a figure of about 5 million (22.5%) by 1990. Though employment in the service sector rose, here, too, private and public sector employers pursued labour economies, especially in the later years of the decade. The process was facilitated by high levels of unemployment which, along with legislative changes, weakened employee and trade union resistance. It fed on rapid developments in information technology which gave significant competitive edge to firms able and prepared to make timely innovations and considerable material rewards to those, the overwhelming majority, who remained in employment. Between 1979 and 1989, labour productivity grew at an annual rate of 1.8% (4.2% in manufacturing), closing but not eliminating the gap between the UK and the USA and European Community (EC)* (where labour productivity remained respectively 33% and 25% greater in 1986) [87, Crafts in 89, Supple in 92] [*Doc. 25*].

Though supply-side developments improved efficiency, economic growth, especially in the years 1985–89, was based on an unprecedented expansion in consumer spending. People saved less; the ratio of savings to personal income fell from 13.5% in 1980, to 8.2% in 1986 and 5.4% in 1988. They also borrowed more, encouraged by an easing of credit regulations early in the decade. Private debt levels doubled from £57 to £114 per £100 of disposable income between 1980 and 1990. Most of this was ostensibly for property purchase, with mortgage debt increasing six-fold in the same period. However, this also represented a degree of 'equity withdrawal' (estimated at £25 billion in 1988 alone), with homeowners diverting resources into other forms of consumption. Such spending was not only on furnishings and consumer durables for the 2 million houses that changed hands in that year, but also on cars, where total UK sales grew from 1.5 million at the beginning of the decade to over 2 million in 1987–89, on other consumer goods (including products of the revolution in information technology), on fashion products or on leisure activities including foreign travel [12, 15 for 1991, 87].

Spending power was enhanced by the number of new jobs created, nearly 3 million, albeit many of them part-time, between 1984 and 1990 (a much better achievement than that of other large EC countries), and, between 1986 and 1990, by a sharp fall in unemployment from 3.4 million to 1.5 million. North Sea oil, from which surpluses were channelled into foreign investment, and a healthy general export performance meant that government did not have a balance of payments problem before 1987. This contributed to some easing of monetary policy. The mid-to-late 1980s boom led to an increase in stockbuilding and in private, though not public, sector investment. Figures for central and local government investment, except in the period 1982–86, continued to decline. Investment by nationalised industries declined appreciably after 1983, though this was largely a by-product of privatisation. By 1990, public sector investment (once nearly half of all investment) represented around 10% of the national total [15 for 1991, 87].

The government had laid great stress on reducing the burden of taxation. In particular, income tax rates had been reduced, especially for the wealthy where the top band was cut from 83% to 40%. This was designed to stimulate supply, by encouraging enterprise, as well as demand. Overall, though, the direct and indirect tax burden grew, especially in the short term, largely because of the social security charges on it. Nor did international evidence support the view that the greater inequalities created added to the rate of economic growth [12, 37, 43].

By 1989, economic indicators were looking grim. GDP growth was only 1%, compared to an average of 4.5% p.a. over the previous two years. North Sea oil production had peaked in 1985–86. The consumer boom had sucked in imports at an expanding rate while exports had failed to keep pace. The balance of payments, in spite of an overseas investment portfolio of £100 billion (second only to that of Japan), was again a problem. Unemployment began to rise. So did inflation, reaching 10% once more during 1990. Base rates, used as a means of maintaining the value of sterling, had been raised to 15% by the autumn of 1989 and stayed at that level until after entry to the European Exchange Rate Mechanism (ERM)* a year later. The effect was to accelerate the downturn in economic activity as consumer spending was diverted into debt servicing, especially the greatly increased mortgage payments that had accompanied the 1980s doubling in house prices [12, 15 for 1991, 87] [*Doc. 26*].

THE 1990s

The slump at the beginning of the 1990s was deeper than that of a decade earlier and, once again, the UK fared worse than her industrial rivals. No other major economic power suffered a year-on-year 2% fall in GDP at constant market prices, as the UK did between 1990 and 1991. Nor, apart from Canada, did any other major country's GDP decline for more than one year. However, just as with the earlier depression, the UK emerged from it sooner than most of her rivals and her subsequent growth was stronger. By 1993, with OECD and Group of Seven (G7)* growth at 1.0%, the GDPs of Germany, France and Italy in decline, and the GNP of Japan expanding by just 0.1%, only the USA, with 2.3% growth, outperformed the 2.1% of the UK. The admittedly not very exciting average of 2.8% GDP growth over the next three years was better than that of any of the other six G7 states and anticipated growth in 1997 (of 3.2%) maintained that situation [*Doc. 28*].

In manufacturing, the decade saw a remarkable turnaround in the fortunes of car manufacture. There was no longer a British-owned volume car-maker, BMW acquiring Rover in 1994. However, substantial investment by Japanese manufacturers, anxious to break into

EC markets, as well as by longer-established multi-nationals like Ford and General Motors, contributed to substantial increases in productivity and production. With sales boosted as states emerged from recession, British output reached 1.64 million in 1996, the highest figure since 1973, with exports taking 54% of production (the first time for more than 40 years that exports had exceeded home sales). Against that, imports still took 62% of the British market of 2 million car sales [5, No. 519].

The dominant characteristic of the 1990s economy has been the continued advance of the service sector and relative decline of manufacturing. It was 1995 before manufacturing regained the output levels attained before the 1990–92 slump. The FTSE–100* index of leading shares, a reflection of economic structure and relative performance, was now dominated by service sector companies, notably those in media or financial services, with floated building societies reinforcing this position. By contrast, when it was first established, in 1984, more than two-thirds of the firms quoted in the index had been in manufacturing. Media played an important part in export performance too, with EMI, for example, having 14% of the world record market in 1995 and music alone contributing £571 million net to the balance of payments, mostly through royalties for live performances and broadcasts.

Figures for employment emphasise the shift in economic activity. By 1995, the country had more health and social workers (974,000) than builders (830,000), while manufacturing had shed 794,000 jobs since 1990. Among individual companies, three of the ten largest employers were in retailing (Sainsbury, Tesco and Boots) and three more were in banking. Overall, by 1996, under 19% of the British workforce was to be found in manufacturing, an indicator not just of shifts in economic structure but of the fact that even successful manufacturing sectors tended to operate with much smaller workforces than hitherto. In this respect, the UK was ranked tenth among EC countries, just ahead of France and Ireland. Germany, with nearly 25% of her labour force to be found in manufacturing, retained the heaviest commitment to this form of employment. Overall, employment figures continued to demonstrate a quest for labour economies, or 'downsizing' as the euphemism had it. Total employment fell by 6.6 % over the three years 1990/91 to 1992/3; its growth after 1993 was at a more modest rate. Here, too, the UK experience anticipated that of other countries with the mid-1990s showing similar sustained reductions in employment numbers, especially in Germany and Italy.

Unemployment once more rose to over 10%, peaking at 10.4% in

1993 before falling to 5% by the end of 1997. Although the UK figure was above the OECD average in the early part of the decade,
there was convergence in the middle 1990s when British unemployment levels, while well above those of the USA and Japan, were
generally below those of other major European countries [5, Nos.
519, 531].

By contrast with the previous decade, the 1990s have seen a constant problem on the external account. At worst, the balance of
payments showed a deficit of over £10 billion in 1992 and 1993 (particularly disturbing given that these were years of relatively low
economic activity). The deficit on goods has remained fairly steady,
with a 44% growth in imports in 1991–95 offset by a 47.3% growth
in exports. A positive balance on services (roughly doubling 1991–
95) and on investment income, where strong growth led to a surplus
of around £8 billion in 1994 and 1995, has been countered by a
deficit on transfer payments of over £5 billion in each of the years
1992–94 and nearly £8 billion in 1995 [5, No. 519].

ACHIEVEMENTS, LIMITATIONS AND EXPLANATIONS

Between 1979 and 1995, the UK's GDP, at constant prices, expanded
by 35.2%. Such a rate of growth was modest compared to that of the
years before 1973, and in some respects remained inferior to that of
other major economic powers. Manufacturing growth over the period
was the worst of any of the G7 economies and unemployment and inflation rates had both proved more volatile than elsewhere. On the
other hand, in a period of generally slower growth and a return to a
cycle of international boom and recession, the 1980s and 1990s saw
a recovery in the relative productivity of British industry, the checking (and in some cases reversal) of decline in some major staples,
good relative performance in high-growth sectors like media and
pharmaceuticals, and continued improved strength in a range of
service industries. The economy had gone through a rather painful
period of adjustment but had emerged in the late 1990s much more
competitive than it had been in the late 1970s.

However, though there had been considerable domestic changes,
the relative position owed much to the lower rates of growth and oc-
casional particular problems of some of the traditionally more dynamic
economies of the post-war era. Germany, France, Japan and others,
all of which industrialised later and all of which had an enormous
amount of recovery to make after the disasters of the Second World
War, were now similarly mature economies. A convergence of

achievement and experience was apparent. Indeed, it was noticeable that the USA, the other laggard among major economies in the post-war years, was now, from time to time, the pace-setter, though at a slower pace than that of the 'tiger' economies of East Asia.

It was also the case that greater manufacturing productivity had been achieved more by shedding employees than by investment in labour or equipment and increased output. The manufacturing sector had shrunk relative to that of services and its share of world trade had resumed a decline that had been checked in the 1970s. Much of what remained was in foreign hands. This was not in itself a weakness. It meant that Britain was attractive to inward investment and it was matched by greatly enhanced British investment overseas. What was more significant, perhaps, was that, at the beginning of the 1990s, labour productivity in foreign-owned companies manufacturing products in the UK was 40–50% higher than in British-owned firms; only about half of this could be explained by the tendency for these multi-nationals to be concentrated in technologically more advanced sectors [15 for 1996, 30] [*Doc. 29*].

British R&D levels remained distorted by defence expenditures, although, largely as a result of defence cuts, the government share had fallen from 33% in the early 1970s to 14% in the mid-1990s. An unusual feature was the 15% of industrial R&D that came from overseas, one of the highest figures among OECD countries. Government policy in the 1980s and 1990s had been increasingly one of providing an environment for research rather than direct funding. Measures included the 1988 Link initiative, encouraging firms to collaborate on pre-competitive research, and the 1993 Technology Foresight Programme, to promote co-operation between industry and the scientific and technological community in identifying technological trends and market opportunity [15 for 1996].

The 1980s and 1990s also saw a host of measures designed to improve the skills levels of the population. There was an increase of almost 50% of those staying in education beyond the age of 16. Successive measures included the Technical and Vocational Education Initiative (TVEI)*, the introduction of National Vocational Qualifications (NVQs)* and General National Vocational Qualifications (GNVQs)*, a national curriculum for schools, the Pick-up Industry Training Scheme*, Enterprise funding* for institutions of higher education, and the introduction of the Investors in People* standard. The employer-run Training and Enterprise Councils (TECs)* and the merging of the employment and education ministries in the Department for Education and Employment (DfEE)were further indications of the growing recognition that Britain's workforce remained under-skilled by comparison with that of her major rivals [12, 15 for 1996].

The financing of British industry continued to be a source of disadvantage. Major banks, while drawing stability from being national and large-scale, lacked the local knowledge and regional commitment of banks in, say, the USA, and also the close involvement with industrial management typical of Germany or Japan. This particularly affected medium- and smaller-sized firms, which continued to find difficulty in borrowing long-term. In a bid to assist investment by smaller companies, which generated twice as many new jobs as larger companies, the government established the Enterprise Investment Scheme and, later, under the 1995 Finance Act, Venture Capital Trusts (VCTs) to provide risk capital for businesses with growth potential. Larger firms tended to have a better relationship with the banks, drawing, like German companies, three-quarters of their external funding from this source. However, during the 1980s, they raised a larger proportion of their total funding needs externally, 30% as opposed to 12% in Germany [15 for 1996, 26].

The need for greater external (and therefore more expensive) funding was a consequence of two interlinked facets of the British economy. British companies distributed a higher proportion of profits as dividends than did their foreign competitors. This was largely a consequence of the high level of shareholding by financial institutions which, if they did not get good returns on their investment, would switch holdings elsewhere, driving down the value of the company. A secondary cause was the way in which the stock market eased hostile takeovers (a phenomenon almost unknown in Germany); high dividends were a way of fighting off predators. The consequence of this diversion of profits was less, or more expensive, investment than competitors overseas [12, 26].

While deficiencies remained, from the viewpoint of the later 1990s, Britain's relative economic position was undoubtedly stronger than it had been two decades earlier. Inflation and unemployment levels tended to be around the median of major international economies. The UK had also performed strongly, particularly in comparison to the rest of western Europe, during the 1980s and 1990s in growth of GDP per head, labour productivity or Total Factor Productivity in manufacturing. For political economists, the issues were no longer why Britain continually lost ground and whether decline was reversible. Now debate turned on whether the 'recovery' was sustainable, given the apparent overwhelming dependence on a strong service sector and the ever shrinking significance of manufacturing, and whether government policies since 1979 had been necessary and sufficient to bring about the present situation [19, 30]. The 1980s certainly saw a change in the ideology governing economic policy. Prioritising monetary targets rather than employment levels had been an innovation, for pragmatic reasons, in the late 1970s; now this became an article of belief, if not always of practice. This policy coincided, and was often incompatible, with measures to free internal and external financial markets. At the same time, legislation and, in the case of the miners' strike of 1984–85, other measures were used to break the power of trade unions. Curtailing the independence and funding of local authorities, enforced competitive tendering and privatisation represented further conscious moves towards an unfettered market economy.

Many of the actions taken were either necessary or had economically beneficial effects. Britain's position in global financial markets demanded removal of controls in that area even if one consequence was the unsustainable debt-funded boom and subsequent bust of the late 1980s and early 1990s. Privatisation freed industries from bureaucracy and from vulnerability to damaging intervention in their investment strategies. In some cases, but not perhaps enough, it led to better levels of service and competitive pricing. Legislation was probably necessary to curb organised labour's power in the workplace.

However, other factors also contributed to the changed economic environment. The effects on the world economy of the second wave of oil price increases, an impact reinforced in the case of Britain's manufactured exports by the soaring value of oil-backed sterling, might well have led to a dramatic elimination of weaker firms and a substantial reduction of manning levels without the reinforcing consequences of the government's tight fiscal and monetary policies of 1979–81. The economic growth of the mid-1980s and again the mid-1990s was shared by other countries not following British policies, nor having the benefits of North Sea oil. Developments in service and competitive pricing are again an international phenomenon, in some sectors not unconnected with massive advances in information technology. Historically high levels of unemployment, and the insecurity that this brought, probably contributed as much as trade union legislation in curbing strike activity, wage demands and restrictions on working practices. The low inflation of the 1990s has again been international, linked to developments in technology and the relative fall in the price of commodities.

Thus, while the measures of British governments between 1979 and 1997 were generally well received by the international economic community (and in some cases imitated by other governments), much of such change as occurred was largely independent of government action. Moreover, there remain two other questions. First, did governments of the 1980s and 1990s simply reassert the primacy of the international financial services industry, where Britain (or London) had long had competitive advantage, over manufacturing, where she had not? Secondly, did the conscious reinforcement of inequality through taxation policy and restrictions on income maintenance benefits achieve economic growth at an unnecessary social price and also, by fuelling expansion but also removing purchasing power in time of slump, aggravate the ferocity of the economic cycle of the decades in question?

6 CULTURE AND DECLINE

Concern over relative economic decline dated, as we have seen, from some time before 1914, although it only became something of a national obsession from the 1960s or 1970s. Earlier chapters have dealt with the economic evidence and how to interpret it. Here, we consider whether, as some have claimed, there are peculiarities in British society that have contributed to economic 'failure' and, indeed, why the issue of decline has attracted so much attention.

Those who propose cultural explanations of decline, suggest that in recent times there has been a hostility to wealth drawn from industry or, to a lesser extent, commerce. Once Britons have wealth, it is argued, they seek the status of landed gentlemen and engage their energies and talents in local or national political activity, the professions or in the financial sector of the economy. Political leaders and the people have sought consensus and security at the expense of economic growth. *Who* has been more important than *what* you know. Even within industry, the long predominance of the family-run firm, lukewarm at best to applied science or professional management, has been an obstacle to technological or organisational innovation and, hence, to optimum economic growth. The British education system, it is claimed, has at once reflected and reinforced this phenomenon; it has failed the economy. Evidence is drawn from literature and the arts, from public speeches, from school records and from the histories of individual families. It is with these issues, especially the uniqueness claimed for the British situation and experience, that this chapter is concerned [Balogh in 3, 27, 56].

Cultural explanations of relative decline date mainly from the post-1960 period when observers sought explanations of the fact that, as with the USA earlier, the economies of western European countries and Japan were overtaking the British in terms of wealth generated and the material living standards of their inhabitants. For some writers, this meant that the longstanding issue as to whether there had been a failure of entrepreneurship became of less importance than that of determining why this might have been, or had been, the case.

ATTITUDES TO BUSINESS

D.C. Coleman, a British economic historian, writing originally in the early 1970s and recalling the old cricketing distinction between amateurs (gentlemen) and professionals (players), explored the likely consequences of a haemorrhaging of talent from industrial families into gentlemanly pursuits and of public school or shop floor origins in business. He accepted that the exodus from business by educated gentlemanly members of financially successful families could have had the invigorating effect of creating opportunities for new generations of 'thrusting, ambitious players', i.e. it was not necessarily to the disadvantage of industry and commerce. However, he suggested that there was evidence that both the public school educated 'amateur' and the self-made 'practical man' were likely to be hostile to applied science or other theoretically based knowledge including management techniques and industrial psychology. Moreover, in the larger companies in which both were present, for reasons of background in the one case or age on reaching the board on the other, both also tended to favour stability and security rather than intensified competition and maximisation of long-term profits.

Coleman assumed neither entrepreneurial failure nor the inappropriateness of a public school education to the overall needs of the country. This education was clearly compatible with success in banking and finance and it also produced first-class administrators who served the country and the empire well. If this was at the price of a degree of industrial advance, it might well have been a price worth paying. In respect of smaller businesses, where there would not usually have been a public school presence, he suggested that cultural explanations of deteriorating performance might require evidence of a decline in the quality of 'practical men' coming forward after about 1870 [27, 28].

Martin Wiener, an American cultural historian, wrote in the context of the deeply disturbing economic experiences of 1973–81, at a time when there were real concerns that the British economy was passing into a downward economic spiral and de-industrialisation. Whereas Coleman was cautious and dealt in alternative hypotheses, Wiener offered a much simpler and more definite picture. His indictment of cultural attitudes struck a chord with the Thatcherite political ideology of the need to change if the country was to reverse a century of decline.

For Wiener, the crisis of the 1970s had been preceded by a century of psychological and intellectual de-industrialisation. From mid-Victorian times, there had been a civilising of English society; it had become more constrained [*Doc. 24*]. Successful industrialists and their families had been absorbed into an established elite of civil servants and financiers, educated together in the developing public schools, mainly with southern and rural locations, and the old universities. These schools and universities disparaged business and produced classically educated administrators and professionals. When secondary schooling was extended in the twentieth century, civil servants ensured that it was in the public school image. Even when, in the 1960s, Warwick University did establish close business links, it was not long before it was being condemned (with some justification) for 'commercial corruption of higher national values'.

The society that emerged from the late nineteenth century was more humane and politically stable than that of the late eighteenth and early nineteenth centuries and it provided greater security and, in time, equality and social legislation. It administered with efficiency the development and later disbanding of a great empire. However, this civilisation, which extended in the twentieth century to a political moderation which compared sharply with much of continental Europe, was accompanied by a condemnation of the evils associated with industrialisation and a generally low status for industry which served to hasten the move from entrepreneur to gentleman.

This society was represented, Wiener claimed, in the literature and other artistic activity that it patronised. There was an idealising of the past, through the Gothic revival and later Morris, and of England as a green and pleasant land. This continued way into the twentieth century with both Labour and Conservative parties having strong leanings towards a rustic and 'traditional' England. Late nineteenth-century criticism of industrial society and of American materialism, as well as what Malcolm Bradbury called a 'deep vein of rural nostalgia', was evidenced in the work of Arnold, Mill, Dickens, Ruskin and Hardy and echoed in the post-Second World War popularity of Betjeman and in J.B. Priestley's emergence as a campaigner against modernisation and change. To sympathetic Americans like John K.Galbraith or Bernard Nossiter of the *Washington Post*, in the 1970s, the British had wisely chosen quality of life in preference to maximum material advance.

For Wiener, the 'English' had chosen a quiet life. Even would-be modernisers like Wilson in the 1960s or Heath in the early 1970s had been thwarted once in office. There were critics. C.P. Snow likened the condition of England to that of the Venetian Republic, unable to break out of existing patterns once the tide of history had turned against it; Lord Nuffield spoke of a 'nation in semi-retirement' in 1959; the novelist Margaret Drabble wrote in despair of 'retreatist' social values in the 1970s. The greatest challenge to Margaret Thatcher would not be in relation to money supply, government spending or reducing trade union power, but in persuading the English to embrace change [56].

Correlli Barnett's *Audit of War*, published during the economic recovery of the mid-1980s, explained Britain's post-war economic 'failure' in similar cultural terms. For Barnett, a military historian turned polemicist, an 'enlightened establishment', middle-class liberals with no contact with the world of industry or commerce, had seized the chance offered by the Second World War to re-shape Britain. However, this establishment, with its deep nineteenth-century roots, rejecting eighteenth-century materialism and rationality in favour of romanticism, emotion and idealism, had diverted national resources from economic regeneration towards the establishment of a social new Jerusalem.

This 'social miracle' incorporated values instilled into different sectors of the population by public schools, universities and nonconformist chapels. It sought to replace 'selfish greed', the supposed legacy of Victorian capitalism, by a Christian community in which individuals were motivated to work for all, the state providing against adversity. In the face of growing evidence of public opinion and media demand for such a reformed society, officials and politicians planned and, after 1945, implemented policies in this vein. The consequence in education was a system which, contrary to early statements of intent, reinforced the old grammar school traditions and neglected the needs of business, technology and design [*Doc. 12*].

For Barnett, prioritisation of social wellbeing, taken alongside a futile but extremely expensive bid to retain great power status in the post-war world, placed an intolerable burden on an already overstrained and inefficient economy which had depended heavily on the USA's support in meeting wartime demands and had, in fact, been out-performed in war by that of Germany in producing the materiel of war. Establishing this liberal social agenda involved, therefore, not only a lost opportunity to re-orientate British institutions in a way calculated to improve relative economic performance in the 'cruel real world', but also placed economy and society under new burdens that aggravated competitive disadvantage [85].

The implication of a 'cultural' explanation of decline is, of course, that Britain is different, in these respects, from other apparently more successful nations and that the cultural norms or needs of the decline period differ from those of earlier years when the British economy was self-evidently the most dynamic in the world.

Use of literary and artistic evidence of an anti-industrialist or pro-rural ethos is susceptible to criticism from a number of perspectives. Germany (Nietzche, Günther Grass, Berthold Brecht), America (Sinclair Lewis, Upton Sinclair) or France (Balzac, Flaubert, Zola) all provide plenty of examples of literary figures hostile or, at the very least, indifferent to industrialism. The Japanese *Samurai* legends, and other artistic dramatic and visual artistic traditions, are hardly indicative of a rejection of the old order and an enthusiastic acceptance of modern industrial society. In Britain, Charles Dickens's *Hard Times,* Mrs Gaskell's *Mary Barton* or *North and South*, or Charlotte Brontë's *Shirley* are all novels critical of the commercial-industrial ethos dating from the period of British economic predominance, as, directly or less directly, is much of the work of Blake, Wordsworth and other Romantic poets. This is not surprising. Historically, literary and other artistic output has been the product of a class with little experience of the industrial world and one which might be expected to reject its essentially materialist values. What cannot be established, however, is that British output is qualitatively or quantitatively more anti-industrial or anti-commercial than that of other countries, or that the views expressed are only characteristic of the years after 1870. Nor is there any evidence that the views expressed in literature or the arts in any way affect attitudes towards engaging in business activity [Robbins, James in 29].

The argument that, from the late nineteenth century, British industrial wealth was increasingly diverted into landed estates and the exercise of political power (the so-called 'third generation' theory) is open to similar criticism. Activity in trade and industry to purchase land and status had always been a characteristic of Britain and other societies; it is not a novel or unusual characteristic of the period from 1870. Nor are land and entrepreneurial activity incompatible. The British aristocracy had always been noted for its profit-orientation and economic innovation; this formed a vital component of the industrialisation process. Nor were old and new money antagonistic. It has been pointed out that successful businessmen like W.H. Smith or Lord Leverhulme found landholding perfectly compatible with continued vigorous entrepreneurial activity and that established landholders have been prominent in business investment [Robbins in 29, 46] [*Doc. 5*].

There was, perhaps, a difference in attitudes to, and involvement in, politics. Successful English businessmen felt obliged to play a role in public life; German entrepreneurs did not and consequently were, from the late nineteenth century, able to devote more time to economic activity and to the particular political interests of their businesses. British political life, it has been argued, is more of a full-time professional business than elsewhere and that has precluded the development of a professional business class. As a result, government, though not hostile to business, has lacked an understanding of, or commitment to, its needs [Robbins in 29, 60].

Sitting somewhat uncomfortably alongside the criticism that British entrepreneurial families abandoned enterprise for land or politics is the argument that the predominance of the family firm, with limited resources and a hierarchy closed to outsiders, was a peculiar weakness of British economic organisation. In fact, Britain and Germany show strong similarities in recruitment of their business elites, with family firms playing a dominant role in the great industries of both countries until late in the twentieth century; Courtauld in textiles and Nuffield in motor vehicle manufacture were matched in Germany by Krupp and Hoecht in steel or Siemens in electrical engineering. Nor were such firms necessarily dysfunctional, hindering new technical and commercial initiatives. While Nuffield, especially in the post-1945 period, might be seen as weak in this respect, the success of other family-owned firms was a reflection of their readiness to adapt and innovate. The breakdown of family ownership in Europe was an international phenomenon associated with the twentieth-century growth of scientific management. It did not occur more slowly in Britain than elsewhere, nor, as the ongoing problems of the BMC and its successors demonstrated after Nuffield, was it a pre-condition of entrepreneurial success [James in 29, Lewchuk in 33, 107].

Contrasts with the USA can also be exaggerated. Here, too, there has been gentrification of wealth and dynastic inheritance. However, developments in management structure have run far ahead of those in Europe. Major reasons for this are the size of the country and anti-trust legislation, introduced at the end of the nineteenth century, which ruled out cartels but allowed single companies to cross state lines. The consequence was a merger movement, particularly between 1898 and 1902. The large-scale, geographically spread companies that emerged needed structured management and made maintenance of family control more difficult. By the 1920s, a divisional structure within organisations was commonplace. A further contrast in circumstances has been held to explain the early attention the Americans gave to distribution and marketing. Whereas major British exports (e.g. cloth, coal, iron and steel, machinery), went largely to other producers where personal contact was as important as marketing skills, American firms were, to a greater extent, selling direct to consumers. Personal contact was impossible; distribution and marketing were all-important [Collins in 29].

THE EDUCATION SYSTEM

The core of the 'cultural critique' of British performance is condemnation of Britain's (or more accurately, England's) education system. This criticism focuses on two overlapping features of provision. One strand suggests that the public schools and, to a lesser extent, the universities took the offspring (in practice, sons) of families engaged in industrial activity and, through the curriculum and the general values instilled, gentrified them, diverting them into non-industrial occupations in administration, the professions or finance. The other strand concentrates on the provision and curriculum of education as a whole, suggesting that, in comparison with other countries, the needs of technology and business have been neglected. There has been a persistent emphasis, at the higher levels, on a humane education, the production of gentleman amateurs, professional men or public servants and, at lower levels, on the production of competent clerks [50, 83, 85].

Both elements of this critique are open to challenge. W.D. Rubinstein, the British social historian, and others have used empirical evidence to undermine the assertion that public schools and universities made gentlemen professionals out of the sons of businessmen. Using the records of a number of public schools, of varying status but admittedly mainly in the south, Rubinstein demonstrated that in the period before 1914 relatively few businessmen sent their sons to public schools but that, in most of the schools examined, numbers did increase over time. More than anything else, though, these were schools for the sons of professional men. However, the number of 'graduates' of these schools going into business was generally greater than the number of sons of businessmen recruited to the school and the pattern, until 1870, was one of increasing numbers entering the business world, though by some calculations the trend tended to be reversed thereafter. The main conclusion to be drawn was that sons tended to follow a similar career to that of their fathers [46, 50].

Nor were these schools responsible for inculcating old aristocratic and anti-entrepreneurial values and styles of behaviour. New nineteenth-century establishments were reformed institutions in terms of curriculum and style and the older public schools were forced to follow their lead. For the social historian, Harold Perkin, this represented a triumph of middle-class values over aristocratic. Nonetheless, they did educate for public service and professional careers, reflecting the backgrounds of most of their intakes. The twentieth century has seen a continuation of this practice, although the professionalisation of business management has meant its assimilation into the professions. In the post-Second World War period, and especially after 1960, these schools reformed themselves again, often giving a lead in technological or enterprise education and stressing individual achievement as much as corporate. Products of these schools (and the universities) have come to dominate all professional and managerial hierarchies. They have, though, continued to favour the financial services or larger corporations rather than traditional manufacturing industry [46].

The universities, especially Oxford and Cambridge, have had an image essentially similar, if exaggerated, to that of the public schools. In the nineteenth century, the sons of businessmen rarely went to university; overwhelmingly the older universities recruited from, and produced graduates for, the professions. Less than 10% of Cambridge entrants 1752–1886 were the sons of businessmen, compared to nearly 33% who were sons of clergymen, while under 4% went on to become businessmen. Evidence for the first half of the twentieth century suggests that, while proportions recruited from families in 'commerce' grew to 32.5% by 1937–38, by 1952 only 17.8% of these undergraduates were subsequently engaged in 'commerce' as a career. The sharp inter-generational decline suggested in these figures could, however, be a reflection of the particular professionally orientated education provided by the older universities [50].

By the end of the nineteenth century, the establishment of Appointments Boards and other reforms at Oxford and Cambridge indicated recognition of a potentially changing market for their graduates, but they and similar institutions in Scotland did not meet the needs of industry. In England, however, new civic universities, as well as other technical teaching institutions, were developing and they had a much closer relationship with industry. These colleges, with financial support from industry, and in some cases owing their very existence to local industrialists, developed industrial research specialisms and sent a great proportion of their graduates into industry. Parallel developments included use of economics as university training for businessmen, where Cambridge, the London School of Economics and Birmingham

Universities took a lead, and research in engineering, electrical physics and shipbuilding, as part of a close involvement with industry in early twentieth-century Scottish universities [51].

During the first half of the twentieth century, war needs (and the loss of German imports) gave a great boost to research in applied science. This was reinforced by trends in industry where electrical and electronic engineering, chemicals and a number of other 'new' industries depended initially on university-based research, and later on university science graduates, for their own research departments. At the same time, the growth of formal and functional management, a development reinforced by middle-class wartime losses, led to a more general demand for university-educated employees, a demand which turned into a veritable 'scramble for graduates' in the 1940s and 1950s.

Post-1960 expansion in higher education has been driven by twin concerns of social justice, allowing all who can to benefit from higher education, and national economic need. Some have doubted, however, that expansion has met economic need. Certainly, it has led to an increase in students and research in applied science and in business and management, and to a much closer involvement with the business world than had been known before. But it has also, it is argued, led to an even larger increase in student numbers and research in the humanities and social sciences, to a degree of academic drift even in science and engineering and to a decline in the overall quality of students undertaking those subjects most directly useful to industry.

The main features of the expansion of higher education in the late twentieth century have been the institution of technological and other new universities following the Robbins Report (1963), the development of polytechnics (the 'new' universities of the 1990s) and diversification of the work of colleges that had previously concentrated on teacher education.

Some of the new universities, for example Sussex, Kent at Canterbury or York, demonstrated no particular commitment to education for industry or commerce; nor, later, did diversifying colleges of education. Other university creations of the 1960s did develop significant business-linked specialisms in areas of work familiar today but novel (and considered with some suspicion) at the time. Electronics at Essex involved close association with Plessey, Marconi and Bell, while the GPO endowed a chair in telecommunications. Lancaster University established Britain's first chair in marketing (funded by the Institute of Marketing) and the 1960s saw, too, the Wolfson Chair in Financial Control. Similar posts were established in commercial systems studies and in behaviour in organisations. Lancaster was also one of the first universities to set up its own consultancy firm as well as playing a leading role in a local initiative to attract new science-based industry to the stagnant economy of north Lancashire. Warwick, more than any other university, set out to establish a close relationship with the business world. Unusually among new creations, it was located close to an important industrial town, Coventry. There were funded chairs in business studies (Institute of Directors), industrial relations (Pressed Steel Fisher), management information systems (Barclay's Bank), forming, with other activity in the fields of economics and computing, a Centre for Industrial and Business Studies. Engineering was another Warwick specialism with involvement from Decca, Bristol Siddeley, Mullard's, Alfred Herbert's and English Electric, and, taking advantage of its location, work in conjunction with the motor industry. Other activities, undertaken in co-operation with local companies, included early work on computer-aided design [51, 98].

Technological universities were generally long-established centres of higher technological learning. They had been known as Colleges of Advanced Technology from 1957. These institutions, including Strathclyde, Salford and Surrey, along with the polytechnics, formed a few years later from regional and other major technical colleges, represented a clear commitment to the development of higher education in the service of industry and commerce. Their range of work was more vocationally orientated than that of most other parts of Britain's higher education system. However, although successive funding methodologies attempted to shape patterns of recruitment, the development of these institutions, particularly that of the polytechnics, both in courses offered and curriculum content, gave rise to accusations of failure to meet the demands of an ailing British economy. Moreover, there existed, until the 1990s, a binary system, with universities funded separately from and more generously than polytechnics and other colleges. This implied a lower status for the latter with consequences for the quality of applicants for their courses and attitudes of employers to their graduates.

The 1960s also saw the establishment of Britain's first business schools. In a bid to concentrate talent, just two national schools were created, in London and Manchester, with the University Grants Committee combining with the independent Foundation for Management Education in raising funds from industry. Later, further funding was raised to establish two more, in Scotland and in the Midlands, in each case co-ordinating and developing work in a number of existing institutions. Numbers of such schools expanded rapidly from the 1970s with virtually every university making similar provision. The result, in many cases, was courses too general to be of use to particular industries, staff with little or no experience of practical issues in the management of British businesses and, in the short term at least, low entry standards leading to graduates of limited management potential [8, 51, 52].

Both old and new institutions of higher education were also affected by a shift in the pattern of qualifications of would-be students. From 1960, when 64.5% of A-level passes were achieved in mathematics or the sciences, the proportion of passes in the arts and social sciences began to grow. In some areas, notably chemistry, there was an absolute fall in applicants for courses, leading to a lowering of standards of entry even in departments of high standing. As early as the end of that decade, the Dainton Report was expressing serious concern at the potential results of these changes for science, technology and management [*Doc. 18*]. By the 1990s, a combination of shortage of applicants, high costs in science and engineering teaching and falling funding in real terms, was leading 'old', 'new' and even technological universities like Brunel to merge or close departments. Developments in the later 1990s indicated recognition of the need for an improved relationship between higher education provision and the demands of an advanced economy. Collaboration between universities and major engineering firms such as British Aerospace, Ford and Unipart in developing courses to meet their specific needs was encouraged by the Labour government's 'University for Industry' scheme, while, on a broader front, the Dearing Report (1997) stressed the need to provide funds to expand higher education providing a flexible, relevantly educated workforce (especially in terms of information technology) with, at the same time, closer involvement of employers with higher education institutions [9, 10, 51].

Supply of students reflected school curricula as well as student choice. At the turn of the century, the scientific, technical and vocational bias of the higher grade elementary schools was rejected by the Board of Education. A balanced curriculum, demonstrating a commitment to literary and classical education, was imposed on secondary schools, while the curriculum for elementary schools stressed an education for life rather than for employment. In the post-Second World War educational settlement, industrial and technological needs, though recognised, were subordinated to action to achieve a settlement of the religious question, the Norwood Committee's commitment to the traditional grammar school curriculum and other politically more pressing demands on government funds [83, 85] [*Doc. 15*].

At school level, it was only in the 1980s and 1990s that government intervened directly in the curriculum to encourage technical and vocational orientation. Then, in the wake of fears concerning de-industrialisation and the lack of employment-related skills, came the range of measures outlined in Chapter 5, several, significantly, funded by the Department of Employment. This belated acknowledgement of the inter-dependence of education and employment skills led, in the 1990s, to the merging of central direction of education and employment in the Department for Education and Employment (DfEE).

Two further and important points need to be made in respect of the numbers passing from the public schools or universities into the world of finance or the professions. The first is that these have been major growth sectors of the economy not just in the twentieth century but throughout the modern era. Entering the professions or other services represented rational career choices on the part of graduates from public schools or universities. The second is that these sectors have generally out-performed industry in the economy. In international terms, for example, whatever the judgement of Britain's industrial performance over the past century, no one seriously challenges the continued importance of London's financial services as one of the major world players. If the public schools and universities have been preparing people for success in that sector, they have certainly been effective in serving national economic need [50].

British education has generally been found deficient in relation to business needs when compared to that of economic rivals; in particular, German and American higher education have been seen as contributing positively to the economic achievements of those countries.

In Germany, the strength of university science and the creation, during the second half of the nineteenth century, of *technische hochschulen* have been seen as indicative of a more positive attitude towards industrial needs. It was certainly true that her education system served Germany well in the scientifically based 'second industrial revolution' of the second half of the nineteenth century, with the chemical, optical, high-grade steel and electrical trades benefiting particularly. However, it would be wrong to assume a harmonious and consistent relationship between German education and German economic needs. By the end of the nineteenth century, German engineers were complaining of a lack of status; *technische hochschulen*, unable to award doctorates until 1899, were not considered the equal of universities, with one survey revealing that they were training only one in six of industrial chemists. At the same time, the supply of chemists far outran national demand. At school level, the practical secondary schools (*realschulen*) were seen as inferior to the academically inclined *gymnasien* [James in 29].

During the first half of the twentieth century, the relationship between German technical and scientific education and business was particularly troubled. Over-supply meant low pay and status for those with scientific and technical training. The inter-war slump aggravated this situation. Under the Nazis, overall university student numbers were reduced, while the removal of Jewish professors and the politicisation of some branches of science did further damage, leading to a 'lost generation of scientists'. After the Second World War, a shortage of scientists and engineers led to a dramatic rise in their status as well as their numbers. This, though, was part of a Europe-wide phenomenon, one in which Britain, up to a point, shared. It was, in part, a consequence of a managerial revolution, opening the boardroom to men (and, though rarely, women) of education and merit [James in 29].

There has been a marked contrast with Britain in the quantity and status of business education provided by American universities. The establishment of the School of Finance and Economics at the University of Pennsylvania in 1881 was followed by a rapid growth of business schools and business degrees. Prestigious institutions, including Harvard and Cornell, were to the fore in this development, as was Stanford, which, from its establishment, was practical in orientation. By 1970, when British business schools were just getting underway, the USA had nearly as many business schools as schools of education. By 1985, American universities and colleges awarded over 223,000 bachelors' degrees in business and management, representing a quarter of all awards and two-and-a-half times the number of education degrees, the next most popular. Master's degrees in Business Administration (MBAs), another American innovation, were also closely associated with high-status institutions. Even in the mid-1970s, Harvard Business School alone was providing around one-fifth of top executives in the largest American companies.

A consequence of this contrast was that senior American business leaders tended to be better and more relevantly educated than their British counterparts. This, in turn, probably did reflect a contrast in cultures. While there is little evidence of an anti-business culture in Britain, there is even less of any pro-business ethic. In the USA, where big government is feared in a way that big business is not, there has long been a competitive ideal, a literature of self-help and later of management, and a tax-encouraged philanthropy, e.g. investment in libraries or educational endowments, that concentrates on encouraging people to perform more effectively [Collins in 29].

Thus, while the anti- or non-business emphasis of British school and university education has been exaggerated, it is the case that economic rivals have tended to be more pro-active and that such education has not enjoyed the prestige, in Britain, that it has had in the USA and, to a lesser extent, Germany. That contrast is, in itself, rooted in cultural and institutional traditions that result from differing economic circumstances. In the USA, a highly educated management, like high capital investment, was a means of overcoming the shortage of skilled workers and of dealing with the large scale of both markets and many firms. In Germany, education, particularly in science and technology, was in part a function of the nature of industrial processes at the time of rapid economic expansion and a means of catching up. Nor should it be forgotten that British education does seem to have served banking and finance well, and that is an area where Britain has long held comparative advantage.

CONCLUSION

While there is some mileage (but probably not a lot) in explanations of performance that centre on disparity in educational provision and, in turn, on those that link that disparity, particularly in respect of America, to a more positive pro-business (though not a pro-finance) culture, there is little to be said in support of other supposed cultural explanations of British 'decline'. An anti-industrial literary and artistic tradition is pervasive to all countries and to the whole of the modern period, and it is not possible to establish any link between such perspectives and economic actions. Traditional elites in Britain were probably more open to enterprise than those of most other countries and they readily assimilated the new rich. Nor have landed estates proved incompatible with continued business success. There may be some significance in the paradox that, while business success in Britain has tended to be accompanied by political obligation, the country has lacked a political business class to press the interests of industry and commerce. This argument is not, however, convincing in respect of financial services, where governments have frequently been accused of putting the interests of the City of London before those of industry.

Historians appear undecided as to whether an inter-generational shift out of industry, insofar as it happened, represented loss or gain. Rubinstein has suggested the shift might be no more than demographic illusion, caused by there being more sons than vacancies in family firms. If there was some loss, it could be seen as a loss of entrepreneurial drive, but, against that, family firms have also been seen as hindering innovation or obstructing the rise of new talent.

Overall, cultural explanations of British economic failure depend, first, on an acceptance of a concept of failure that is far from consistent or proven, second on an over-simplified interpretation of the role of British institutions, especially educational institutions, and finally on a distinction between British and foreign cultural contexts that, for the most part, is hard to sustain.

PART THREE: ASSESSMENT

Previous chapters have demonstrated that concerns about decline have varied over the period since 1914. On the eve of the First World War, the economic foundations of Victorian prosperity appeared secure; criticism focused on Britain's performance, relative to that of other countries, in newer, science-based industries. Only the USA and Germany were seen as serious rivals. During the inter-war years, it was the staple industries, the pillars of the old industrial order, that did badly. Moreover, decline in the output of industries like cotton and coal was absolute and, it began to appear, irreversible. By contrast, performance in newer industries was better, not only than that of the older staples, but, in some cases, than that of similar industries abroad. By the later 1930s, in spite of the ongoing problems of some industries and regions, there was a degree of optimism about Britain's overall economic condition.

The achievements of the Second World War, and artificial world economic conditions of the late 1940s, did little to dent that optimism, nor was there serious concern as the economies of other countries, especially in western Europe, grew more rapidly throughout the 1950s. Britain's own growth record was impressive by historical standards, trade was buoyant, there was full employment and living standards remained the best in Europe.

The issue of decline achieved a new importance in the late 1960s and in the 1970s. There was a sharp deterioration in the balance of payments. Per capita output and living standards in other European countries caught and then surged ahead of those of the UK. 'Old' and 'new' industries alike ran into serious difficulties. Unemployment returned. Serious problems of inflation were cause and consequence of a serious decline in the value of sterling. Improved statistical data and changing concepts of the state's economic role and responsibilities, both in part a product of the Second World War, contributed to a noisy debate as to the extent, cause and solution to the 'crisis'. By the late 1970s, the economy had become the most important political issue and some commentators were arguing that Britain's economic decline was terminal. The position after the slump of 1979–82 changed markedly. Economic growth, particularly in western Europe, was much slower than in the preceding three decades. Britain, while subject to extreme fluctuations of boom and slump and in sterling values, and to sustained high levels of unemployment, had an economic record which was at least comparable with those of major competitors. By the late 1990s, the economic debate centred on the potential problems of a two-speed economy, with services vastly out-performing manufacturing, on the sustainability of growth, and on the over-valuation of sterling. In a manner reminiscent of 1914, critics warned against an over-optimistic interpretation of present conditions; there was an apprehension that the economy was not equipped for longer-term optimum performance. All this, though, was a far cry from the gloom of the 1970s [12, 99].

The British economy of 1914 was highly competitive in the context of contemporary world markets. In longer-established sectors, it depended, to a greater extent than competitors, on a plentiful supply of skilled labour but this was an area where British producers had a comparative advantage. Limited investment in new technologies was also a consequence of heavy investment in still efficient older plant and equipment or their lack of suitability for the nature of goods being produced. In a number of cases, failure to invest in new and labour-saving technologies would aggravate long-term difficulties for British industry, but much of the decision-making had been economically sound in the context of pre-First World War conditions.

A similar contrast between short-term advantage and future problems can be identified, with hindsight, in respect of the structure of shipbuilding and other industries. Foreign tariffs and competition had led to increased concentration on imperial markets and this, the tendency to lag behind in products with a high scientific or technological input, and specialisation at the lower end of international markets were, again, indicators of limited future potential.

Domination of overseas investment markets, as well as those of insurance and shipping, served to reinforce the demand for other British goods and services. There is no evidence that the outflow of capital was at the expense of domestic investment or standards of living. Indeed, the strong performance of service and consumer goods industries suggested quite the opposite. Overall, the position in 1914 was healthy and Britain still held a position in the world economy out of all proportion to her size and resources. Much of what had happened and was to happen was a corrective adjustment of an inevitably temporary and artificial situation. The First World War accelerated that process. Exports were curtailed and world capacity developed. Industries where Britain had been dominant lost market share. Conversely, 'new' and science-based industries benefited from the artificial protection of war and from government initiatives, then and later, to encourage their development. The post-war world, the new international financial order and government monetary measures in the face of this may have aggravated, but were not the fundamental cause of, the sectoral and regional difficulties that were a particular feature of the 1920s.

Inter-war experience was broadly a contrast between that of industries and services catering primarily for a home market that was either naturally or tariff protected and that of industries heavily dependent on depleted demand from overseas. Among industries targeted on home markets, science and technology-based industries, and others catering for a new mass market in consumer products, did better than pre-1914. Among older export-orientated staples, while managerial and entrepreneurial failings sometimes reinforced difficulties, the root problem lay in the collapse of external demand and could not be resolved by firms trapped in a web of debt and deficient sales. Natural economic forces combined with industry and government-sponsored rationalisation to shift resources out of declining staples, but the extent of this by 1939 was not sufficient to eliminate unemployment and idle plant [*Doc. 10*].

Criticism of government policy appears misplaced. The return to, and subsequent abandonment of, the gold standard had little deleterious effect. Indeed the commitment to order in exchange rates during the 1920s and the safe monetary policies of the 1930s may well have encouraged economic activity. Rationalisation activities, in which government was directly or, more commonly, indirectly involved, were restricted more by industrial resistance than by weakness of policy. Regional policy was half-hearted, but post-1945 experience hardly suggests this was a cure for the scale of localised economic problems in the 1920s and 1930s and it is anachronistic to condemn governments for not implementing Keynesian counter-cyclical macroeconomic policies before they had been properly formulated.

Indicators of economic growth, over the inter-war period as a whole, compared favourably with those of the pre-1914 era but less well with those of most economic rivals. Convergence continued. However, 1929–38 relative performance was much stronger and by

the end of the period the USA was still the only country to outper-
form the UK in GDP per head [*Doc. 25*].

While there is a need to acknowledge the contribution of the USA
to the British war effort, 1939–45, and the peaks of mobilisation
achieved by Germany and the USSR, Britain's balanced and sustained
mobilisation for war was without parallel. The war was costly in
terms of Britain's long-term resources and relative economic position,
particularly in relation to the USA. Against that, it represented gains
in respect of economic statistics and understanding of the economic
role and potential of governments.

The post-war climate of economic management and of increased
commitment of resources to education and welfare was beneficial to
economic growth. So was the world-wide pent-up demand for capital
and consumer goods. Britain was initially well-placed to benefit from
this demand but the emphasis was on restoring markets and meeting
demands, on production rather than productivity or investment in future growth. There was an initial over-concentration on sterling
markets, not the wealthiest, but also, and more positively, on products in which trade was developing most vigorously.

The 1950s and 1960s saw a sustained record of economic growth
which surpassed that of even the 1850s, 1860s and early 1870s. It
was also a period of full employment and marked increase in real incomes. Other countries, however, did better. Initially, this could be
assigned to post-war reconstruction, higher levels of population
growth and a belated move of workers from low productivity agriculture into manufacturing and services. However, these factors did not
account for UK per capita GDP falling below that of the OECD as a
whole by the end of the 1960s. One important reason for this was the
substantial diversion of resources into an international military role
that was beyond the country's means. A resulting deficit on the government external account put pressure on the balance of payments,
leading to deflationary policies to defend sterling. Research and development funds were also over-committed to a narrow range of
defence-related activities. The subordination of an industrial strategy
to immediate political economic priorities in the case of nationalised
industries was another contribution by government to relative economic under-performance.

How bad were the 1970s? Looking back, the decade certainly appears to have been economically turbulent and one when some old
fears returned. It was a decade of external economic shocks and of internal disruption. Perhaps more than anything else it was a decade of
forced, if unrecognised adjustment. Joining the EEC simply reflected

a growing inter-relationship of the British and western European (and, incidentally, American) economies and a relative decline in the significance of trade with the old and new commonwealth. The decade saw increased imports (particularly of manufactures) and, in spite of marketing deficiencies, of exports in relation to domestic output. The assumption that economic fluctuations could be managed, and inflation and unemployment kept under control, was found to be false. Whatever the interpretation of the overall record of industrial relations, management of labour and capital was revealed as flawed in important sectors of the British economy. But this was a difficult decade for all industrialised states. In fact the decade was a turning point but not in the way it was portrayed at the time. The 1970s did not see British manufacturing industry enter a phase of terminal decline. Rather, the decade saw the gap between British economic performance and that of major rivals begin to narrow.

Economic performance during the last two decades of the twentieth century contrasted sharply with the earlier post-war era. Extremes of boom and slump accompanied governments committed, in principle, to reducing the role of the state in economic matters and to creating an enterprise economy. A corollary of this policy was to free employers from some of the influence on employment and work practices exercised by trade unions [*Doc. 24*].

Some of the 1970s experiences were encountered again in more extreme form: unemployment at times exceeding 3 million; a huge and permanent shake-out of labour from manufacturing industry; international speculation leading to wild fluctuations in the value of sterling. These, though, were now accompanied by political messages that such developments were the price of upgrading the economy, restoring competitiveness and international confidence or, when sterling rose, a response to what had been achieved.

The British economy did perform relatively better. Although inflation generally remained above the median for major industrial nations, the British record was not noticeably bad, and by the middle and late 1990s there was optimism that the problem had been conquered. GDP growth over the period was marginally above that of the EC taken as a whole. The productivity gap was closed. British investment overseas built up and Britain became, by a distance, the major EC beneficiary of inward investment.

In part, both beneficial and less welcome elements in the changed situation were the result of government policy. Credit liberalisation fuelled the 1980s boom but reinforced the slump of 1990–92. Direct and indirect curbs on trade unions contributed to greater efficiency in the use of labour but contributed to a harsher climate for employees and much higher unemployment. North Sea oil provided income and some protection from the vagaries of world fuel markets but had much to do with a damaging surge in the sterling exchange rate at the beginning of the 1980s . Together these factors did contribute to the turnaround in Britain's relative position. But other influences on British performance have owed little to government ideology. No industry or service was immune to the effects of information technology on labour requirements and productivity. Falling commodity prices, worldwide, had a lot to do with reduced inflation. The increased integration of advanced international economies has encouraged convergence.

The view that unique cultural factors have contributed to Britain losing ground to economic rivals has little to commend it. It is hard to identify a general exodus from successful business families into politics and landholding, but, even where this has happened, there is little evidence that it has proved incompatible with successful entrepreneurship. Nor is it certain that such an exodus, clearing the way for new talent, would necessarily be detrimental to economic performance. The existence of anti-industrial cultural perspectives, as represented in literature or the arts, is hardly peculiar to Britain, or to the period of supposed decline; nor is it possible to establish a link between such attitudes and economic behaviour.

There is, perhaps, a problem, in Britain, of combining business and political interests with the effect that the country lacks a business political interest. The result may have been government which, while not hostile to business, has tended to be indifferent to, or ignorant of, its needs.

The notion that the education system has not served industry well may also have some substance. Management and technological education were slower to develop and tended to lack the status they held in the USA, Germany or France. Public schools and the older universities provided much better for the professions, including financial services (which were, in fact, the major growth sectors), than they did for industry. The contrast should not be over-stated. There were perceived problems of status for much technological education in Germany in the earlier twentieth century; no one would claim the American education system is without fault. Scottish and English civic universities always had closer links than Oxbridge with industrial demands. But there were and are deficiencies. Even in the 1990s, there is a perceived shortage of young workers with skill qualifications and major companies are turning away from institutions to offer an appropriate education to their workforces.

So how should we judge British economic performance since 1914? At the beginning of this book, it was pointed out that any idea of decline was one which had to accommodate a five-fold increase in GDP and one which left the vast majority of the population in the 1990s living at a level of affluence unimaginable a century ago. Moreover, in spite of an apparent increase in social and economic divisions over the past 20 years, people live with much greater state-provided security than at the beginning of our period; few (albeit still too many) live, as the American writer Jack London found them at the beginning of the century, on the edge of (or in) 'the abyss'.

There has undoubtedly been a relative decline. Britain, as another and anglophile American Bill Bryson, somewhat bemused at the national obsession with failure, has recently pointed out, is 'a small island'. She is no longer able to exploit a vast empire. In terms of overall output, she has inevitably fallen behind larger and intrinsically richer countries like the USA, Germany and France. But this does not explain why per capita GDP should have fallen behind that of much of western Europe (tenth among EC members in 1995). This decline can in part be explained by geography. As in pre-industrial times, Britain is very much on the edge of the European economic area, and there are built-in disadvantages to this and to being an island. It is no accident that the part of the UK closest to the European mainland, the south-east, has been the most dynamic part of the British economy for much of the twentieth century. Slower growth can also be ascribed in part to the economic make-up of the UK. The very success of Britain's nineteenth-century economy left vast resources tied up in slow-growing and declining sectors for much of the century. Poor management training and a desire to avoid disruption of production when demand was buoyant in the 1950s and 1960s probably contributed to the scale of difficulties in the 1970s, while lack of adequate skills training and marketing failings have dogged Britain's industry (but not its service sector) for much of the century.

Actually, the artificiality of treating states as single economies has long been recognised. All countries contain industries and regions that have had to face painful adjustment at different times in the twentieth century; the UK perhaps, because of its inheritance, simply had more of these. Alongside her declining manufacturing industries, by contrast, she has maintained a healthy service sector, with London, in particular, remaining a major world force in financial services.

However we measure the UK economic condition and wellbeing in relation to the G7 nations or the other members of the EC, we should remember that these are clubs containing the richest of the world's states. The gap between the UK and those within these groups with stronger economies is much less than that between the UK and the great majority of the world's nations. Britain remains one of the world's economic elite (indeed has been seen as a model European economy for competitiveness in several recent surveys). To adapt a quote from yet another American, Mark Twain: report of its economic death was an exaggeration.

PART FOUR: DOCUMENTS

DOCUMENT 1   THE TRIUMPH OF FREE TRADE

The Economist, the great advocate of free trade, applauds the performance of British industry in the decade to 1912.

At the end of the nineteenth century, foreign competition with Great Britain reached its most acute stage, alike in the home and neutral markets. English business men seemed to be wedded to traditional and conservative methods, both in manufacturing and marketing. Our markets seemed to be inundated with goods 'made in Germany'; American bicycles and boots were to be seen everywhere. But with the new century, our manufacturers and merchants woke up to the situation: the tariff reform agitation forcefully called attention to the condition of affairs; men of business began to look into German and American methods, technical and vocational education was improved, the Board of Trade developed its Commercial Intelligence Department, and this revival, stimulated by foreign competition, and working with all the advantages of cheap production, achieved ... stupendous results.

The American bicycle was driven off the market, the American boot has lost its hold, the British clock has recaptured its market, the motor trade has grown up and is pushing its sales abroad. The great staple trades are more prosperous than ever before. To a large extent these results are attributable to the rising cost of production abroad, thanks to American and German tariffs; but in some measure this extraordinary triumph of Free-trade may be attributed to an expansion of business intelligence in reply to Mr Chamberlain's raging, tearing propaganda.

The Economist, 11 January 1913.

DOCUMENT 2   HEGEMONY THREATENED

A year later, the same journal observes that, while 1913 has been a record year for shipbuilding, Britain's share of world output is declining.

A spell of shipping prosperity often begets a shipbuilding boom; for when freights are high and shipping profits large, owners are encouraged to build. And as the United Kingdom is the predominant shipbuilder of the world, the statistics of British shipbuilding yards often follow a few months behindhand the trend of shipping and general trade activity. These generalisations are certainly true of the particular year 1913, in which the output of British yards has easily created a record. But remarkable as [the] British figures are, the rest of the world has increased its output even faster. The United Kingdom still builds more mercantile tonnage than the whole of the rest of the world put together, but whereas in 1911 she was responsible for 68% of the world's merchant tonnage launched, this figure fell to 60% in 1912 and 58% in 1913. Comparison between the output of the United Kingdom and that of other countries for the past eight years is as follows:-

Year	The World (tons)	United Kingdom (tons)	Other countries (tons)
1906	2,919,763	1,828,343	1,091,420
1907	2,778,088	1,607,890	1,170,198
1908	1,833,286	929,669	903,617
1909	1,602,057	991,066	610,991
1910	1,957,853	1,143,169	814,684
1911	1,650,140	1,803,844	846,296
1912	2,901,769	1,738,514	1,163,255
1913	3,332,882	1,932,153	1,400,729

The Economist, 31 January 1914.

DOCUMENT 3   LOST OPPORTUNITY

The electrical engineering industry was one where Britain had fallen behind America and Germany. A Board of Trade committee, reporting in 1918, suggests why.

Through the efforts of Faraday, Wheatstone, Kelvin, Swan, Hopkinson and many others, Great Britain was, and should have continued, first in electrical enterprise ... In order, however, to bring electrical energy into practical use, it was necessary to employ cables, either underground or overhead, the installation of which involved interference with streets, roads and private lands. Manufacturers of electrical equipment had been held back while Parliament and local authorities debated how the distribution and use of electricity might be prevented from infringing conventional conceptions of public privilege and vested interests ... While America, Germany, and other countries were eagerly seizing the benefits of electricity, our authorities were busied with the erection of obstacles to its development ... but there was another factor, namely, that in the initial stages foreign countries possessed a pioneering advantage in that their general industrial progress had not reached so high a degree of development as had Great Britain in the application of steam engineering. Great Britain, on the other hand, had undoubtedly attained great prosperity and technical efficiency in her use of steam plant, and there was therefore less inducement for her manufacturers to adopt electrical driving ...

Another retarding factor regarding electrical progress in Great Britain has been the strength of the gas interests and the influence they exerted to stifle competition.

Board of Trade Departmental Committee on the Electrical Trades, *Report*, Cd 9072 (HMSO, 1918) pp. 3–7.

DOCUMENT 4   **MISGUIDED POLICY**

John Maynard Keynes criticises the policies associated with a return to the gold standard at $4.86 in 1925.

The Bank of England is *compelled* to curtail credit by all the rules of the gold standard game. It is acting conscientiously and 'soundly' in doing so. But this does not alter the fact that to keep a tight hold on credit – and no one will deny that the Bank is doing that – necessarily involves intensifying unemployment in the present circumstances of this country. What we need to restore prosperity today is an easy credit policy. We want to encourage business men to enter on new enterprises, not, as we are doing, to discourage them. Deflation does not reduce wages 'automatically'. It reduces them by causing unemployment. The proper object of dear money is to check an incipient boom. Woe to those whose faith leads them to use it to aggravate a depression!

J.M. Keynes, [13] p. 220.

DOCUMENT 5   DIMINISHED VITALITY

The Liberal Industrial Inquiry of the late 1920s suggests that the problems of the basic industries are compounded by poor leadership of second or third generation entrepreneurs.

We think that there is in some cases a certain amount of remediable inefficiency within the industries themselves. In certain sections of the coal, textile and steel industries those upon whom responsibility lies seem to outside observers to have proved themselves unequal to dealing with the new problems which confront them. For example, a failure year after year to deal with the problem of surplus capacity and a continued acquiescence in the wastes of working many plants partially instead of securing the economies of concentration does not seem creditable to the powers of initiative and adaptation of those controlling them. Though there are striking exceptions, coal-owners as a class are becoming a proverbial type of conservative obstinacy in the face of changing facts. Even in these cases, however, the inefficiency often lies not in the technical equipment and management of the individual enterprise, but in the policy and statesmanship of the industry as a whole in the face of changing circumstances. This is probably in some degree a natural consequence of diminished vitality in industries which were in their prime and in the forefront of progress two or three generations ago. Then the leaders of these industries were nearly all pioneers; now few of them have reached their present position by their own unaided abilities, but partly at least because they are the sons of their fathers or the grandsons of their grandfathers. Furthermore, the problems of surplus capacity in the face of stagnant or declining demand are of an essentially different character from those of a period of rapid and continuous expansion.

Liberal Party, *Liberal Industrial Inquiry, Britain's Industrial Future* (Ernest Benn Ltd., 1928) p. 42.

DOCUMENT 6   WAGE COSTS AND INDUSTRIAL
             DEPRESSION

Both at the time, and more recently, economic commentators blamed excessive wage costs for lost markets and therefore unemployment in the 1920s.

Let us review the costs which have either risen disproportionately, or not fallen proportionately, in relation to commodity prices. The first and most important is wage-rates. Before the war the policy of maintaining wage-rates in spite of unemployment could be practised only by the organised minority of wage-earners. The majority were unable to resist reductions that were needed to maintain employment; and any workers excluded by the policy of the stronger unions could compete for employment in industries in which wages were not held above absorption level. Today there are no unorganised industries in this sense; wages are held up generally, either by trade union or Government support through statutory wages boards, and workers excluded from employment by a general holding up of wage-rates above absorption level have no resort except unemployment relief. Before the war, again, in the absence of any general unemployment relief, it was impossible to maintain wage-rates generally at a level that restricted employment throughout industry; somewhere, usually at many points, wages (in relation to efficiency) would be reduced to the level at which expansion could take place; the condition 'in relation to efficiency' is necessary, because, in fact, expansion took place in the high-wage rather than the low-wage industries. Today trade union negotiators can afford to take the risk that a wage-rate on which they insist will cause unemployment, because their constituents will be provided for by the national relief scheme.

Even if the union negotiators were under the same compelling incentive to take account of unemployment as they were before the war, there are factors in the wage situation that would lead them to resist reductions. Wage-rates are already lowest by pre-war standards in the industries suffering most from unemployment, and highest in the industries suffering least. To ask miners, steel workers or skilled engineers to accept further reductions, when already their rates are below those of lower grades of skill in sheltered industries, is to invite opposition.

Henry Clay, *The Post-war Unemployment Problem* (Macmillan, 1929) pp. 154–5.

DOCUMENT 7   LANCASHIRE NEEDS A NEW APPROACH

The cotton industry's production methods had served it well in the past. This extract from a report of a committee of the Economic Advisory Council suggests that American and Japanese production and marketing methods were more appropriate to current market conditions.

As it is obvious what trade Lancashire has lost, so it is almost equally obvious how it has been lost. Its successful rivals produce and market cheap staple lines in bulk. Often they use cotton which is good enough for them and their customers but has not been thought good enough by Lancashire. The operatives in India, China and Japan work for long hours at low pay. In the United States especially, expensive automatic machinery, with a high production-capacity to the weaver, is run for many more hours in the week than are the ordinary looms in this country.

... the success of Lancashire's competitors, and, in particular, of Japan, has been due to their being able to manufacture cotton goods and market them at prices substantially less than those of competing goods made in Lancashire. The Japanese product may not be as good as that of Lancashire, but is sufficiently good to satisfy the requirements of the markets in which it is sold. To cheapen manufacture by long runs of the same design, Japan has linked marketing to production and established a rational control over her industry. The Japanese industry has been handicapped by higher capital costs, but it has had a lower wage level, double-shifts, longer hours worked by labour, proximity to markets, monetary conditions favourable to export and lower social charges upon industry. Similar advantages are, or have been, enjoyed by a number of other competing countries.

Economic Advisory Council, *Committee on the Cotton Industry Report*, Cmd 3615 (HMSO, 1930) pp. 11–12.

DOCUMENT 8   **MAKING THINGS WORSE**

The Economist *condemns the National government of the 1930s, claiming that it has aggravated the obstacles to trade resulting from economic nationalism.*

No fair-minded person will lay upon the shoulders of the government the blame or responsibility for the present appalling volume of unemployment, which shows no sign of decreasing. Nor does anyone expect either a miracle or panacea from the Treasury bench. The real charge against the government is not that it has failed to cure unemployment, but that almost every action it has taken since it came into office, both in the domestic and the foreign spheres, has been calculated to aggravate the distresses from which the country is suffering. As Sir Herbert Samuel justly points out, everybody admits that the present conditions of industrial depression are due chiefly to the world situation and to the frantic effort of each and every country to stifle international trade by an indiscriminate throttling of imports. If the world goes on in its present mad course, Mr Chamberlain's pessimism will be more than justified. But what has the National Government done to make things better? What contribution has it made to the lowering of world tariffs? The answer, unfortunately, is less than nothing. In spite of every warning, it has persisted in the dangerous policy of casting out devils by Beelzebub. It has fastened on the country the Ottawa agreements, the only tangible effect of which is to increase the level of world tariffs and to prevent their being lowered by agreement; it has introduced quotas for meat and is threatening to extend them, as part of our permanent economic machinery, to other products; and it has met the only practicable attempt at lowering tariff barriers initiated by Belgium and Holland with a sterile negation, by insisting on the rights of Great Britain under the most-favoured-nation clause.

The Economist, 25 February 1933

DOCUMENT 9   BUILDING THE HOME MARKET

Lloyd George's pamphlet on economic reconstruction suggests that the home economy offers ample scope for economic growth in the 1930s.

But so long as the policy of other countries is wedded to ideas of 'economic nationalism', our chief field for industrial expansion must lie within our doors and within the vast confines of the Empire. In both directions, there is obviously immense scope.

At home the nation is as yet far from being adequately housed, clothed, fed and supplied all round with a reasonable standard of comforts and amenities. In view of the immense increase in our capacity to produce wealth which has been furnished by the application of mechanical power, it is impossible to set a limit upon the upward movement of the general standard of life which the citizens not only of this country, but of the world, might reasonably expect to enjoy.

This process is continually going on. The home market quickly learns to establish new demands and absorb new conveniences – witness, for example, the rapid spread of radio apparatus in the last ten years.

In addition to the large field for expansion in the direct production of saleable goods for the home market, there is great scope for improving the services and amenities of the community ... The clearance of slums and provision of adequate housing accommodation would furnish a valuable addition to the Nation's prosperity, and to its health and efficiency. The improvement of roads and of bridges, docks, harbours and canals would increase the national wealth by facilitating its business and removing costly delays and inconveniences. Improvements of water supply, of drainage and sanitation, of electricity and gas, would enrich the nation in terms of its health and working capacity. A revival of agriculture would bring into profitable cultivation wide areas now under-cultivated or derelict.

D. Lloyd George, *Organising Prosperity* (Ivor Nicholson & Watson, 1935) pp. 21–2.

DOCUMENT 10   GENERAL PROSPERITY

The Economist greets 1937 with an account of the prosperity experienced by most of the country during the previous year.

Anybody who attempts this New Year to assess the outlook for 1937 must first of all take account of the truly astonishing recovery which Great Britain has enjoyed in the past four years. Last year has shown as rapid progress as any of its predecessors. The total of employment in December was almost 5% higher than it had been twelve months before. What is more, the labour force of the nation is being even more effectively used than the bare figures of employment would show; for *The Economist* Index of Business Activity, which is a measure of the whole economic tempo of the nation, has been some 7% higher in the latest three months than in the same period last year. Perhaps the most encouraging aspect of the last year has been the extent to which recovery has spread to many of the basic industries which ever since the war have been among the most depressed. The production of steel in the United Kingdom, for example, was more than 18% higher in 1936 than in 1935. Moreover, imports of iron and steel increased while exports fell off, so that domestic consumption was no less than 27% higher. These are astonishing figures when the period is as short as a year and the circumstances those of an already well-established recovery. Of the four great erstwhile depressed industries – coal, cotton, iron and steel, and shipbuilding – the latter two must now be struck off the list. The Special Areas have experienced some improvement, but in most of them it has served to lighten the blackness of their outlook only to the lightest shade of grey, and there are other districts, such as parts of Lancashire, which are hardly behindhand in depression. But these are the exceptions. The greater part of the country is prosperous to a degree it does not realise and would not have believed possible four years ago.

The Economist, 2 January 1937.

DOCUMENT 11   MOVEMENTS IN GDP 1913–48 (1913=100)

An index of the GDPs of major countries, 1913–48, shows the UK economy losing ground in the 1920s and holding its own in the 1930s. Year-on-year peacetime decline is represented in bold type.

	UK	USA	Germany		UK	USA	Germany
1913	100	100	100	1930	**111.1**	**147.5**	**119.4**
				1931	**105.4**	**135.2**	**110.3**
1919	100.9	115.8	72.3	1932	106.2	**117.1**	**102.0**
1920	**94.8**	**114.7**	78.6	1933	109.3	**114.7**	108.4
1921	**87.1**	**112.1**	87.5	1934	116.5	123.7	118.3
1922	91.6	118.3	95.2	1935	121.0	133.6	127.2
1923	94.5	133.9	**79.1**	1936	126.5	152.7	138.4
1924	**98.4**	138.0	92.6	1937	130.9	160.2	153.4
1925	103.2	141.2	103.0	1938	132.5	**152.9**	169.1
1926	**99.4**	150.4	105.9	1939	133.8	165.0	182.7
1927	107.4	151.9	116.5				
1928	108.7	153.6	121.6	1945	154.5	312.8	145.3
1929	111.9	163.0	**121.1**	1946	**147.8**	**252.9**	**83.0**
				1947	**145.6**	**245.6**	101.9
				1948	150.2	255.0	120.8

Estimates adjusted to exclude effects of frontier changes.
A. Maddison, [41] pp. 214–15.

DOCUMENT 12   PLANNING FOR PROSPERITY

The Second World War demonstrated the role government could play in regulating the economy. In 1941, Picture Post published one of the most celebrated statements on the world that must follow the war. As part of this, Thomas Balogh indicates the need to plan for peace.

The most important thing is to realise that the end of the war will not be a time to return to what used to be called 'normal' – that is, complete freedom for the speculator to make high profits out of the world's need of reconstruction. On the contrary, the reconstruction must be planned exactly as war production ought to be planned. Just as Government controls are needed at present to enable the nation to throw its whole strength into the war, so a system of Government controls – reformed both in character and personnel – is needed to enable us to throw our whole strength into the peace effort. Man-power must be controlled so that it can be directed where it is most needed, and demobilisation must take place not as it did last time

– where millions of men were thrown on to the labour market – but according to the work which can be provided. The supply of materials must be adjusted according to the task. In fact, we must have a national plan of reconstruction. Now the word 'plan' is somewhat unpopular, especially since it denotes a certain amount of compulsion or direction which is not favoured by a freedom-loving people. But we have surely reached the stage of overcoming this prejudice, which has been fostered by people who want freedom to profit at the expense of the majority …

We must also control investment. This must be extended not merely to investment in houses or fixed plant, but also in working capital. At the same time, it will be necessary for the community as a whole to undertake investment should individual initiative fail …

It also means a co-ordinated price and wage policy, with tribunals to enforce equity and prevent hardships … And insofar as the minimum standard of social and health services cannot be secured by appropriate management of investment and wages – and in many instances it cannot – direct subsidies will be necessary.

Thomas Balogh, 'Work for All', *Picture Post*, 4 January 1941 pp. 12–13.

DOCUMENT 13 **NEEDS MUST**

The Second World War necessitated liquidation of overseas assets and the taking on of increased external debts. This transformation of Britain's external account contributed to post-war economic difficulties. Figures are in £ million.

	Sept–Dec. 1939	1940	1941	1942	1943	1944	Jan.–June 1945	Total
Realisation of external capital assets	58	164	274	227	189	143	63	1,118
Increase in external liabilities	80	179	564	519	647	608	282	2,879
Decrease or increase (-) in gold and $US reserves	57	474	-23	-75	-150	-99	-32	152
Unallocated	17	-6	5	3	3	11	16	49
Total in £ million	212	811	820	674	689	663	329	4,198

Central Statistical Office [88] p. 225.

DOCUMENT 14   **WAR AND VISIBLE TRADE**

*Britain had had to fight the Second World War without regard for the
economic future. The excess of visible imports over exports had widened
greatly. Immediate post-war circumstances were, however, favourable to
readjustment.*

In 1936–38 Britain incurred an average annual deficit of £44 million ...
From September 1939 to the end of 1945 the annual deficit averaged about
£700 million, and but for Lend-Lease would have been much more. This
war-time deficit resulted from a deliberate policy – only made possible by
the willingness of a number of countries to accumulate large sterling
balances – of cutting exports to a minimum and concentrating our
maximum productive effort on war requirements. In the words of Lord
Keynes, 'we fought this war on the principle of unlimited liability and with
more reckless disregard of economic consequences than others more
fortunately placed' ... by 1943, our commercial exports had fallen to 29%
of their 1938 volume, while by 1945 they had recovered only to 45%. At
the same time, there was a considerably less drastic reduction in the volume
of retained imports (excluding munitions), which fell in 1942 to 70% of the
1938 level, rose to 80% in 1944, and dropped again to 63% in 1945.
   Although these figures exclude munitions, they reflect a highly abnormal
situation and it would be a mistake to draw too many conclusions from
them. Nevertheless, they do indicate the considerable ground which has to
be recovered merely to restore exports to their pre-war level. It [is]
suggested that at least until the end of 1948, selling prospects will be
particularly favourable for our exports.

Political and Economic Planning (now the Policy Studies Institute), *Britain
and World Trade* (PEP, June 1947) p. 55.

DOCUMENT 15   **TECHNICIANS AND CRAFTSMEN NEEDED**

*In a climate of growing international competition and the increasing
scientific and technological needs of industry, a government white paper
outlines the range of skills required.*

We face, then, an intense and rising demand for scientific manpower and by
no means only for men and women with the highest qualifications. Every
technologist relies on technicians and craftsmen to translate his plans into
products. It would be a great mistake to increase the output of technologists
without adequately supporting them at the lower levels from which in any
event many of them are drawn. Much therefore depends on strengthening
the base of the pyramid of technical education by improving the education

in the schools and raising the numbers of school-leavers who are able and willing to take successfully the courses offered at technical colleges ...

Technical education must not be too narrowly vocational or too confined to one skill or trade. Swift change is the characteristic of our age, so that the main purpose of the technical education of the future must be to teach boys and girls to be adaptable. Versatility has been the aim of a classical education; technical studies should lead to a similar versatility and should, therefore, be firmly grounded on the fundamentals of mathematics and science. It is much easier to adopt new ideas and new techniques when the principles on which they are based are already familiar.

The range of technical education goes far beyond the study of materials and mechanics. Accountancy, costing, salesmanship, commercial skills of all kinds, including foreign languages, are equally important to a great trading nation.

Technical Education, Cmd 9703 (HMSO, 1956) pp. 4–5.

DOCUMENT 16   THE CHEMICAL INDUSTRIES IN THE 1950s

By the 1950s, Britain's chemical industries were among the strongest in Europe. In sharp contrast with the post-First World War era, when they had sought protection, they now saw opportunities in the free internal market which the Common Market would represent.

Because the chemical industry can achieve substantial economies of scale, and because it costs so much to discover and develop a new product or process, the large firm in every European country usually has a distinct advantage over the small. The strength of the British chemical industry is, therefore, best measured by comparing ... the relative sizes and rates of growth of the largest chemical producers. In the countries that compete most closely with Britain in chemicals – in Germany, France, Italy and Switzerland – large firms predominate ... But in none of them is the large firm quite as dominant as it is in Britain. The three largest German chemical firms, Bayer, BASF and Hoechst ... account for barely a third of the turnover of the German chemical industry – about the same proportion as that held by ... ICI in Britain. No German firm can muster capital resources comparable to those of the Royal Dutch-Shell group and other major producers of petroleum chemicals in Britain. The share of output in the hands of the large firms in France and Italy is also less than it is in Britain, and the share of the more vulnerable smaller firms correspondingly greater.

In other respects the record is not so favourable to Britain. Although ICI's sales in 1956 were slightly greater than those of the three largest German chemical producers combined, the German companies' sales were increasing more than twice as fast as ICI's. While ICI exported from Britain chemicals to the value of over £73 million ... the three German firms sold nearly £140 million abroad. ... This exceptional emphasis on export markets, especially in Europe, puts German firms in a strong position to penetrate into the vulnerable French and Italian markets when they lose their tariff protection. In the petroleum chemicals field, however, ... the long lead established by the British and British-Dutch oil companies puts Britain in a position to share with America most of the advantages from the expected growth in European demand.

Economist Intelligence Unit, *Britain and Europe* (Economist Intelligence Unit Ltd, 1957) p. 167.

DOCUMENT 17   SCIENCE, TECHNOLOGY AND THE ECONOMY

The incoming Labour government of 1964 believed that the economic future lay in high technology. The Party's election manifesto indicated the ways in which, in government, it would encourage technological advance.

If we are to get a dynamic and expanding economy, it is essential that new and effective ways are found for injecting modern technology into our industries.

The Government provides over half the money spent on industrial research and development in Britain. Some of this research is already carried forward, in Government establishments like the National Research and Development Corporation set up by the last Labour Government, to the point of commercial development. This has already led to scores of new products and processes of which the Hovercraft and Atlas Computer are only the most famous.

But to get more rapid application of new scientific discoveries in industry, new measures are urgently required. A Labour Government will:

(i)   Go beyond research and development and establish new industries, either by public enterprise or in partnership with private industry.
(ii) Directly stimulate new advance by using, in the field of civil production, the Research and Development contracts which have hitherto been largely confined to military projects.
(iii) Set up a Ministry of Technology to guide and stimulate a major national effort to bring advanced technology and new processes into industry.

Labour Party, *Let's Go with Labour for the New Britain* (1964) pp. 9–10.

DOCUMENT 18   **THE NEED FOR MORE SCIENTISTS**

A government report of the late 1960s suggests that the output of schools needs to be tailored to the increasing demands of industry for highly educated scientists and technologists.

The investigations we have undertaken show clearly that while the output from the sixth-forms of the secondary schools is continuing to grow rapidly, the output of specialists in science is not ... the remarkable growth which has been achieved over the past decade in sixth-form education has been largely devoted to the development of studies which, under present conditions, in effect disqualify for higher education in science and technology.

Against this situation must be set the increasingly important role of science and technology in everyday affairs and in the economy. Discovery and invention in these fields, and their exploitation, depend on an adequate force of scientists and technologists and their effective use in employment. This country, to a greater extent than many others, depends on its qualified manpower as a national resource for the creation of wealth. High level scientific and technical jobs form the fastest growing occupational group in Great Britain ...

In such a situation ... we think it right to insist that the individual, in choosing the subjects that he studies at school, should have as mature an appreciation of those subjects and of the implications for his career as it is possible to give. National requirements do, after all, determine the opportunities for individuals. We feel strongly that considerations of curriculum organisation which have remained substantially unchanged in the last forty to fifty years should not force a premature and largely irrevocable decision for or against science and technology.

GB, [9] (Dainton Report) p. 84.

DOCUMENT 19   **FOREIGN CAR IMPORTS**

Lord Stokes, chair and chief executive of British Leyland Motor Corporation, comments on foreign manufacturers' growing share of the British car market.

I have said elsewhere that those who buy foreign cars need their heads examining ... I do not think they are better than our cars ...   Generally speaking, our experience is that spare parts and the servicing of them is very much more expensive. What they have had is something that we have lacked, and that is availability. We have lost 150,000 cars a year due to industrial disputes, and so on. With regard to our dealers or distributors, the position is just beginning to change now, but for the last five years none of them have had complete availability of motor cars. This has made it very difficult for them to sell. There is no doubt that people will not wait for a motor car for a year or 18 months if there is another car available. ... We have lost dealers that we would have liked to have kept, and could have kept if we had the cars to go through them. They were attracted by getting foreign cars. Once you get it established, people have a traditional loyalty. Also I think probably in this country we have a sort of peculiar attitude. If ... anything is foreign, we seem to think it is better, even if it is not. Quite a number of people who have bought foreign cars have become disillusioned because they have found the very faults they complained of on British cars are there, sometimes to a greater degree, in the imports. On the other hand, I think we have to expect this position. We sell overseas about 50% of our total sales, and we would like to have an environment at home where we can continue to make and sell cars in the home market and for the export markets. I do not think we have ever particularly been advocates of stopping other people coming into the market but we would like to have the same conditions in our market that they have. If you take the Japanese for instance, it was only in the Sixties that the Japanese market was opened up for imports. If we had had a protected home market until the Sixties we would have a much healthier industry than we have today.

House of Commons Expenditure Committee, [11] pp. 121–2.

DOCUMENT 20   FALLING PROFITS, RISING WAGES

Britain's recovery from the slump of 1974–75 was slow. While this report sees government policies as contributing to this, it also suggests that inflation, falling profits and rising real wages and salaries have played a significant role.

While the restrictive policy stance in 1976 and in the first three quarters of 1977 helps to explain the slow recovery from the recession, other factors have also been important. One of these concerns the sharp acceleration in the rate of inflation in the two years to mid-1975 and the persistence of comparatively high rates up to the present. ... Associated with this development was a massive change in factor income shares. Over the two years to end-1975, the share of wage and salary income in national income increased by four percentage points to 69%. The counterpart to this movement was in profits; the share of trading profits of industrial and commercial companies, after allowing for stock appreciation and capital consumption, fell from 7.3% in 1973 to 3.2% in 1975. Although the profit share had been on a falling trend since the mid-1950s, the rate of decline quickened sharply after 1969 when a clear acceleration in the underlying rate of inflation became evident. By international standards, the profit share in the United Kingdom is extremely low, not only recently but over an extended period.

Despite the fall in output and the unprecedented rise in prices, average earnings in real terms rose on average by about 3½% in 1974 and 1975 and the gap between the changes in real wages and productivity widened markedly. ... Not only does [this] adversely affect competitiveness, but it also distorts resource allocation through its effects on investment. Accordingly, it can over time result in a slower growth of output, particularly in manufacturing, and because of its effects on competitiveness give rise to imbalances in trade flows through excessive import growth.

OECD, [15 for 1979] pp. 31–3.

DOCUMENT 21   **SET THE MARKET FREE**

Sir Keith Joseph argues for political action to cure Britain's economic problems.

The delayed and damaging consequences of formal and institutionalised incomes policies are now well known. We have experimented with different arrangements of more or less rigid control of pay for about 20 years. During that time, inflation has reduced the value of the pound by over 75%. Unemployment has nearly trebled, yet industry reports skilled labour shortages. Our share of world trade has fallen sharply. Business profits as a share of GNP have fallen catastrophically. Real take-home pay has been almost stagnant. Over the same period, virtually every one of our competitors has left us far behind, despite the impact of OPEC price rises and in many cases without our advantages of North Sea gas and oil; and without using pay controls. Almost every year, we have produced a smaller share of the world's goods and a larger share of its banknotes. Our problem today is the same as it was 20 years ago, but writ larger: 'We want other countries' goods more than they want ours.'

When we look at the evidence, do we believe that without all those attempts at government controls, we would have done even worse? I suggest that the reality is much simpler. The reality is that, if we had emulated the more successful economies, in monetary policy, labour relations and the scope given to the workings of the market, we would have done much better.

The difference between Britain and other advanced industrial economies is as much political as it is economic.

Sir Keith Joseph, *Solving the Union Problem is the Key to Britain's Recovery* (Centre for Policy Studies, February 1979) pp. 4–5.

DOCUMENT 22   WAS IT LOW INVESTMENT?

In the late 1970s, a committee, chaired by the ex-Prime Minister Lord Wilson, investigated the recurring issue of the relationship between the investment policies of financial institutions and economic growth.

There are many explanations for the relative decline of the UK economy, prominent among which are the relatively low level of real investment in this country, particularly in manufacturing, and the poor effectiveness with which new investment is used. The part that financial institutions have played in this, or could play in helping the economy to break out of the vicious circle, is a matter of contention. In this respect it may be useful to remind the reader – as we have been reminded – of the situation at the time of the Macmillan Committee, which like ourselves was specifically required to examine finance for industry. Our environment and that at the time of the Macmillan Committee share similar features of world recession, low profits, low demand, low investment and a relatively high exchange rate, with one obvious exception that prices were falling in 1931. The words used by some members of the Macmillan Committee describe the late 1970s rather well:

'Today, however, the main trouble is not a limitation on the amount of available bank credit, but the reluctance of acceptable borrowers to come forward'.

Committee to Review the Functioning of Financial Institutions, [Wilson] *Report*, Cmnd 7937 (HMSO, 1980) pp. 19–20.

DOCUMENT 23   THE INDUSTRIAL SPIRIT TAMED

An American, Martin Wiener, writing at a time when Britain appeared faced with economic crisis, argues that this was the outcome of a century of revolt against industrial values.

At the time of the Great Exhibition of 1851, Britain was the home of the industrial revolution, a symbol of material progress to the world. It was also the home of an apparently triumphant bourgeoisie. Observers like Carlyle and Marx agreed in pointing to the industrialist as the new aristocrat, a figure that was ushering in a radically new culture. Yet they were misled. From the time of their assertions, social and psychological currents in Britain began to flow in a different direction.

By the nineteen-seventies, falling levels of capital investment raised the spectre of outright 'de-industrialisation' – a decline in industrial production outpacing any corresponding growth in the 'production' of services. Whether or not such a spectre had substance, it is true that this period of recognised economic crisis in Britain was preceded by a century of psychological and intellectual de-industrialisation. The emerging culture of industrialism, which in the mid-Victorian years had appeared, for good or ill, to be the wave of the future, irresistibly washing over and sweeping away the features of an older Britain, was itself transformed. The thrust of new values borne along by the revolution in industry was contained in the later nineteenth century; the social and intellectual revolution implicit in industrialisation was muted, perhaps even aborted. Instead a compromise was effected, accommodating new groups, new interests, and new needs within a social and cultural matrix that preserved many of the values of tradition. Potentially disruptive forces of change were harnessed and channelled into supporting a new social order, a synthesis of old and new. This containment of the cultural revolution of industrialism lies at the heart of both the achievements and the failures of modern British history.

Martin J. Wiener, [56] pp. 157–8.

DOCUMENT 24   **PRACTISING WHAT THEY PREACHED**

In power, the Conservative government of 1979–83 attempted to eliminate disincentives to economic initiative. The Party's 1983 election manifesto set out what it had sought and achieved.

We want to see an economy in which firms, large and small, have every incentive to expand by winning extra business and creating more jobs. This Conservative Government has been both giving these incentives and clearing away the obstacles to expansion: the high rates of tax on individuals and businesses; the difficulties facing small firms trying to grow, and the self-employed man trying to set up on his own; the blockages in the planning system; the bottlenecks on our roads; the restrictions on our farmers and fishermen; and the resistance to new ideas and technologies.

In the last four years, British firms have made splendid progress in improving their competitiveness and profitability. But there is some way to go yet before this country has regained that self-renewing capacity for growth which once made her a great economic power, and will make her great again.

Only a government which really works to promote free enterprise can provide the right conditions for that dream to come true ...

We have reduced the burdens on small firms, especially in employment legislation and planning and cut many of the taxes they pay. ... Our Loan Guarantee Scheme has already backed extra lending of over £300m. to about 10,000 small firms. The new Business Expansion Scheme ... will encourage outside investment in small businesses by special tax reliefs. ...

Thanks to these policies and over one hundred other important measures, the climate for new and smaller businesses in the UK has been transformed and is now as favourable as anywhere in the world.

Conservative and Unionist Party, *The Challenge of Our Times* (1983) pp. 18–19.

DOCUMENT 25   COMPARATIVE PRODUCTIVITY, 1913–89

This table of GDP per man hour (measured in 1985 $US) shows how Britain first of all lost ground, and then was overtaken by competitors during the post-war years. It also reveals, perhaps surprisingly, the relatively modest achievements of Germany and Japan.

	Belgium	France	Germany	Italy	Japan	UK	USA
1913	2.85	2.26	2.32	1.72	0.86	3.63	4.68
1929	3.80	3.30	2.89	2.38	1.48	4.58	6.88
1938	4.17	4.25	3.57	3.12	1.83	4.97	7.81
1950	4.79	4.58	3.40	3.52	1.69	6.49	11.39
1973	12.79	14.00	12.83	12.82	9.12	13.36	19.92
1987	19.86	21.63	18.35	18.25	14.04	18.46	23.04
1989			19.53		15.18	18.55	23.87

Figures adjusted to exclude the impact of territorial changes.

A. Maddison, [41] pp. 274–5.

DOCUMENT 26   THE END OF THE 1980s BOOM

The overheated late 1980s economy was followed by recession at the beginning of the following decade. This report suggests that the severity of that slump may well have been the result of a delayed response to high interest rates.

Domestic demand fell in the second half of 1990, lowering real GDP growth for calendar 1990 to 0.6%. The fall started with a cut-back on interest-sensitive components of expenditure. New car sales plummeted by some 16% from their year earlier levels in the last quarter of 1990, compounded by higher petrol prices and uncertainty related to the Gulf conflict. Residential housing and related consumer durables were also depressed by sharply increasing debt service and deteriorating household balance-sheet positions. A drop in house prices and an easing in financial market prices quickly turned the cut-back in spending into recession, with

Building Societies reporting sharp increases in mortgage defaults. Indeed, the striking feature of the recession was that private consumption fell, even though nominal wage increases sustained real disposable income gains.

The drop in private consumption and high interest rates worsened already heavily geared corporate balance sheets, and the Gulf conflict increased private sector uncertainty. With corporate profits under sharp pressure and rising bankruptcies, business investment was scaled back in the second half of 1990. Investment in the manufacturing and non-residential construction sectors, where over-capacity and over-building had emerged, had been cut back significantly. However, in marked contrast to previous recessions the scale of de-stocking was quite small, reflecting tight management of inventory levels and the trend towards lower stock/output levels over the past 20 years.

The sharp fall in domestic demand, when it eventually came in mid-1990, was far sharper than expected by almost all observers – suggesting that the effects of interest rates on private expenditure may now be more powerful due to higher personal sector gearing. Financial market liberalisation may well have increased the volatility of private sector expectations.

OECD, [15 for 1991] pp. 15–18.

DOCUMENT 27   INDEX OF GDP AT FACTOR COST,
              1948–96 (AT 1990 PRICES)

This data shows GDP to have more than trebled in the period 1948–96, but also a more volatile performance in the past quarter century. Year-on-year decline is represented in bold type; figures in brackets are for GDP in £ billion at current prices.

1948	34.3 (10.4)	1965	56.6	1982	77.4
1949	35.6	1966	57.6	1983	80.3 (261.2)
1950	36.9	1967	58.9	1984	81.9
1951	37.6	1968	61.5 (37.9)	1985	85.2
1952	37.9	1969	63.0	1986	88.6
1953	39.3 (14.9)	1970	64.2	1987	92.7
1954	41.0	1971	65.3	1988	97.3 (401.2)
1955	42.5	1972	67.2	1989	99.4
1956	43.0	1973	72.2 (65.7)	1990	100.0
1957	43.8	1974	**71.2**	1991	**97.9**
1958	**43.7** (20.2)	1975	**70.6**	1992	**97.4**
1959	45.5	1976	72.5	1993	99.6 (548.0)
1960	48.0	1977	74.4	1994	104.0
1961	49.3	1978	76.4 (149.5)	1995	106.9

1962	50.1	1979	78.5	1996	109.5
1963	52.0 (27.1)	1980	**76.9**		
1964	55.0	1981	**76.0**		

Economic Trends Annual Supplement 1996–97, No. 22 (HMSO, 1996), [5
No. 529, December 1997].

DOCUMENT 28   COMPARATIVE GROWTH IN THE 1990s

*Figures of year-on-year percentage growth of GDP at constant market
prices show the UK, after the deep slump of 1990–92, faring better than the
other major economies of western Europe, but generally less well than the
USA.*

	UK	Germany	France	Italy	USA	Japan	Canada
1990	0.4	5.9	2.6	2.1	1.3	5.2	-0.3
1991	-2.0	no data	0.8	1.1	-1.0	4.0	-1.8
1992	-0.5	1.8	1.2	0.6	2.7	1.0	0.8
1993	2.1	-1.1	-1.4	-1.1	2.3	0.1	2.1
1994	3.9	2.9	2.9	2.1	3.5	0.6	4.2
1995	2.4	2.1	2.2	2.9	2.0	0.9	2.3
1996	2.1	1.3	1.3	0.7	2.4	3.7	1.5

Note Figures for Germany are for West Germany in 1990 and for unified
Germany from 1992; Japanese figures are of GNP.

[5, No. 524, July 1997] p. 12.

DOCUMENT 29   PUTTING OUR FAITH IN THE JAPANESE

*During the later 1990s, British exports stood up well in spite of a sharp rise
in the value of sterling. Here, an economic commentator ascribes this to
generally buoyant world trade. Car exports reflect long-term investment
commitments by Japanese manufacturers and are, therefore, expected to be
sustained.*

Dire warnings have been sounded on the effects of sterling's strength on
Britain's visible trade, stirring memories of old-style balance of payments
crises.

While a widening trade deficit is now almost certain, two points stand
out. First is the evident resilience of export growth to date, and second is

the different order of magnitude compared to previous trade deficits.

Growth in global demand has been helping exporters to cope with the loss of edge on pricing brought by the higher pound. The world economy grew by 2.6% in 1996 and is set to hit 3.2% this [year], providing a partial offset.

A striking change since the 1970s and 1980s has been the performance of car exports. Production for export has climbed from 187,500 in 1986 to 908,200, a near five-fold rise. Much of this reflects overseas, particularly Japanese, investment in the UK. And the game plan of this investment is long term, with the Japanese unlikely to be blown off strategic course.

Bill Jamieson, 'Economic Agenda', *Sunday Telegraph*, 3 August 1997.

GLOSSARY

Balance of payments A country's international account, including visible and invisible trade (see below), but also income from overseas investments and the government's international payments or receipts.

Cartel An association designed to maintain prices and/or market shares for a product or group of products, e.g. in the international chemicals industry in the 1930s or among petroleum-exporting countries in the 1970s.

Dollar gap The gap between income from exports to North America and the much larger expenditure on imports from that area and other regions demanding payment in dollars. In the late 1940s, a world-wide imbalance between American exports and imports led to an international shortage of dollars. In these circumstances, other countries increasingly demanded dollars rather than sterling in payment for British imports and the UK was not able, as previously, to offset a deficit on North American trade by multilateral settlement of accounts. In consequence, there was a drain on Britain's dollar reserves.

Enterprise funding Government funds made available to higher education institutions in the 1990s to promote the development of employment skills within the curriculum.

European Economic Community/European Community (EEC/EC) Essentially a free trade area within a tariff wall. Originally, from 1958, it comprised six states (West Germany, France, Italy, Belgium, Holland and Luxembourg) with the UK, Denmark and Ireland becoming members from 1973. Other states joined in the 1980s and 1990s.

Exchange Rate Mechanism (ERM) Agreement by member states of the European Community to pursue policies to restrict fluctuation of their currencies against one another within a given band. The UK, which only joined the ERM in October 1990, was forced to withdraw in September 1992.

FTSE-100 The *Financial Times* weighted arithmetical index, started in 1984, of the equity shares of the 100 largest companies quoted on the Stock Exchange.

General National Vocational Qualification (GNVQ) See *National Vocational Qualification* below.

Gold standard A situation where a country's central bank is required to provide a given quantity of gold in return for its currency. This means that there is a fixed rate of exchange between all currencies on the gold standard and international debts are settled in gold. The US dollar was the cornerstone of post-First World War arrangements and the dollar remained convertible into gold until the system was abandoned in 1976.

Gross Domestic Product (GDP) The total value of goods and services produced within a domestic economy, including that by companies etc. which are wholly or partially foreign owned and excluding any product of investment etc. abroad. GDP at factor cost is the product value less indirect taxes but including any subsidies.

Gross National Product (GNP) The total value of goods and services produced at home and abroad excluding income from domestic product that accrues to foreign-based investors.

Group of Seven (G7) Seven major industrial economies: USA, Canada, Japan, Germany, France, UK, Italy. From 1998, Russia became a member of G8.

Healey, Denis Chancellor of the Exchequer in the Labour governments of 1974–79. Forced, in the wake of an acute balance of payments crisis and a falling pound, to apply to the IMF for a loan of $3.9 billion. In preparation for this application, and in response to conditions laid down by the IMF, the post-war Keynesian policy of using monetary policy to combat unemployment was abandoned.

Horizontal integration A merger between two firms in the same business, e.g. Austin and Morris in motor vehicle manufacture in 1952 or Granada and Trust House Forte in hotels and catering in the 1990s (see *Vertical integration* below).

International Monetary Fund (IMF) Established from 1947 to encourage international collaboration in monetary matters, rejecting the economic nationalism of the 1930s. The original objectives were to stabilise exchange rates, remove foreign exchange restrictions and to encourage the development of a multilateral payments system between member countries. Member states contribute to the fund, which also has borrowing powers, and draw on it in times of financial need.

Investors in People A form of kite-marking available to organisations able to demonstrate appropriate procedures for developing the capabilities of their employees.

Invisible trade See *Visible trade* below.

Keynesian economic management Government management of aggregate demand as a means of manipulating the level of real output in the economy and, by this means, regulating unemployment. The means used are fiscal (i.e. use of taxation, variations in public expenditure) or, to a lesser extent, monetary (influencing the amount of money in the economy).

Lend-Lease War and other essential supplies provided by the USA during the Second World War, including more than $16 billion in munitions or other goods for the UK and a further $5 billion in ships and services. Payment in dollars was not required but the US President had, in theory, the right to demand payment at some stage.

Ministry of International Trade and Industry (MITI) Japanese government ministry, particularly active in the 1950s and 1960s in shaping the structure of the national economy and the development of a powerful position in international trade.

National Economic Development Council (NEDC) Established in 1962 as a forum for long-term planning. It was chaired by the Chancellor of the Exchequer, included representatives of employers' associations and the Trades Union Congress, and was serviced by officials of a National Economic Development Office.

National Vocational Qualifications/General National Vocational Qualifications (NVQs/GNVQs) Qualifications at different levels, introduced from 1992 under the auspices of the National Council for Vocational Qualifications and designed to develop skills and knowledge appropriate to employment. NVQs are specific to particular trades or industries; GNVQs are broader based.

Organisation for Economic Co-operation and Development (OECD) Established in 1961, growing out of the Organisation for European Economic Co-operation, formed in 1947 to co-ordinate Europe's post-war programme of economic recovery. The OECD is a forum for international economic discussion and provides statistical data and commentaries on the economic performance and potential of member states.

Organisation of Petroleum Exporting Countries (OPEC) A cartel of oil producers, mainly located in the Middle East. OPEC attempts to fix production quotas and prices for the exports of member states. It was at its most influential in the mid-1970s when member states provided some 90% of total world exports. However, the subsequent development of other producers and of substitute fuels undermined OPEC's position.

Pick-up Industry Training Scheme Department of Employment-funded scheme for promoting short courses for industry in institutions of higher education.

Sterling area Countries using the pound sterling for international payment purposes.

Technical and Vocational Education Initiative (TVEI) Launched in 1983 and managed, significantly, by the Manpower Services Commission, part of the Department of Employment. Provided funds for schools and colleges with the aim of reforming the curriculum to bridge traditional boundaries between academic and vocational subjects and providing an education of greater relevance to industry.

Total Factor Productivity (TFP) A collective measure of those inputs to economic growth not covered by the traditional definitions, capital and labour. TFP includes technical change, improvements in human capital (e.g. education or training levels), improvements in the organisation of labour or industrial relations, effects of government policy. Modern economic theory treats this group of inputs as the most important influence on economic performance. TFP indicates rather than explains changes in factor inputs. It can be used to indicate fruitful areas of investigation when seeking to explain economic performance.

Training and Enterprise Councils (TECs) Set up in 1990 on a regional basis to administer government spending on training and to develop area schemes for getting the unemployed into work, utilising private training agencies as appropriate. TECs had a majority of business representatives on their boards and a business person as chief executive.

Vertical integration A merger between firms which have a supplier/customer relationship, e.g. W.H. Lever's acquisition of the Niger Company in 1920 as a means of ensuring raw material supplies for margarine and soap manufacture or British Motor Corporation's acquisition of the car body builders Pressed Steel Fisher in 1966.

Visible/invisible trade Visible trade is in goods (e.g. textiles, cars, ships, aircraft, oil); invisible trade is in services (e.g. banking and insurance, tourism, provision of air or sea transportation). Historically, the UK has run a deficit on its visible trade and a surplus on invisibles.

BIBLIOGRAPHY

Place of publication is London unless otherwise stated.

PRIMARY (i.e. WORKS ABOUT THE PERIOD IN WHICH THEY WERE PUBLISHED)

1   Allen, G.C., *The British Disease: A Short Essay on the Nature and Causes of the Nation's Lagging Wealth*, Institute of Economic Affairs, 1979.
2   Bacon, R. and Eltis, W.A., *Britain's Economic Problem: Too Few Producers*, Macmillan, 1976.
3   Blackaby, F.T. (ed.), *De-industrialisation*, Heinemann Educational, 1979.
4   Bowker, B., *Lancashire Under the Hammer*, Leonard and Virginia Woolf at the Hogarth Press, 1928.
5   Central Statistical Office GB, *Economic Trends*, HMSO.
6   Coates, D. and Hillard, J., *The Economic Decline of Modern Britain*, Harvester Wheatsheaf, Brighton, 1986.
7   Coates, D., *The Question of Decline*, Harvester Wheatsheaf, Brighton, 1993.
8   Franks, Oliver, *British Business Schools*, British Institute of Management, 1965.
9   GB, *Final Report into the Flow of Candidates in Science and Technology into Higher Education* (Dainton), Cmnd 3541, HMSO, 1968.
10 GB, National Committee of Inquiry into Higher Education (Dearing), *Higher Education in the Learning Society*, HMSO, 1997.
11 House of Commons Expenditure Committee, *The Motor Vehicle Industry: Report and Minutes of Evidence* 617, 617/1-III, HMSO, 1975.
12 Hutton, W., *The State We're In*, Vintage, 1996 edn.
13 Keynes, J.M., *Collected Writings*, Vol. IX, *Essays in Persuasion*, Macmillan, 1972 edn.
14 Manser, W.A.P., *Britain in Balance: The Myth of Failure*, Longman, 1971.

15 OECD Economic Surveys, *The United Kingdom*, OECD, Paris.

16 Pollard, S., *The Wasting of the British Economy*, Croom Helm, 1982.

17 Singh, A., 'UK industry and the world economy: a case of de-industrialisation', *Cambridge Journal of Economics*, 1: 2, pp. 113–136 June 1977.

18 Sked, A., *Britain's Decline: Perspectives and Problems*, Blackwell, Oxford, 1987.

19 Smith, K., *The British Economic Crisis*, Penguin, Harmondsworth, 1989 edn.

20 Rostas, L., 'Productivity of labour in the cotton industry', *Economic Journal*, 55, pp. 192–205, 1945.

21 Rostas, L., *Comparative Productivity in British and American Industry*, Cambridge University Press, Cambridge, 1948.

22 Thirlwall, A.P., 'De-industrialisation in the United Kingdom', *Lloyds Bank Review*, 144, pp. 22–37, April 1982.

23 Williams, K., Williams, J. and Thomas, D., *Why are the British Bad at Manufacturing?*, Routledge and Kegan Paul, 1983.

SECONDARY (i.e. WORKS WHICH ARE HISTORICAL IN THEIR EMPHASIS)

General works covering the period before and after 1939

24 Aldcroft, D.H., *The British Economy*, Vol. I, *Years of Turmoil 1920–1951*, Harvester Wheatsheaf, Brighton, 1986.

25 Alford, B.W.E., *Britain in the World Economy since 1880*, Longman, 1996.

26 Capie, F. and Collins, M., *Have the Banks Failed British Industry?*, Institute of Economic Affairs, 1992.

27 Coleman, D.C., 'Gentlemen and players', *Economic History Review*, 2nd series, 26: 1, pp. 92–116, February 1973.

28 Coleman, D.C. and MacLeod, C., 'Attitudes to new techniques: British businessmen 1800–1950', *Economic History Review*, 2nd series, 34: 4, pp. 588–611, November 1986.

29 Collins, B. and Robbins, K. (eds), *British Culture and Economic Decline*, Weidenfeld and Nicolson, 1990.

30 Crafts, N., *Britain's Relative Decline 1870–1995*, Social Market Foundation, 1997.

31 Deane, P. and Cole, W.A., *British Economic Growth 1688–1959*, Cambridge University Press, Cambridge, 1969 edn.

32 Dintenfass, M., *The Decline of Industrial Britain 1870–1980*, Routledge, 1992.

33 Elbaum, B. and Lazonick, W. (eds), *The Decline of the British Economy*, Oxford University Press, Oxford, 1986.

34 Feinstein, C.H., *National Income, Expenditure and Output of the United Kingdom, 1855–1965*, Cambridge University Press, Cambridge, 1972.

35 Floud, R. and McCloskey, D. (eds), *The Economic History of Britain since 1700*, Vol. II, *1860–1970s*, Cambridge University Press, Cambridge, 1981.

36 Furner, M. and Supple, B., *The State and Economic Knowledge*, Cambridge University Press, Cambridge, 1990.

37 Gamble, A., *Britain in Decline: Economic Policy, Political Strategy and the British State*, Macmillan, 1994 edn.

38 Kirby, M., 'Institutional rigidities and economic decline: reflections on the British experience', *Economic History Review*, 2nd series, 45: 4, pp. 637–60, November 1992.

39 Landes, D., *The Unbound Prometheus*, Cambridge University Press, Cambridge, 1969.

40 Layard, R. and Dornbusch, R., *The Performance of the British Economy*, Oxford University Press, Oxford, 1988.

41 Maddison, A., *Dynamic Forces in Capitalist Development. A Long-Run Comparative View*, Oxford University Press, Oxford, 1991.

42 Matthews, R.C.O., Feinstein, C.H. and Odling-Smee, J.C., *British Economic Growth 1856–1973*, Oxford University Press, Oxford, 1982.

43 Middleton, R., *Government versus the Market*, Edward Elgar, Cheltenham, 1996.

44 Mitchell, B.R., *International Historical Statistics: Europe 1750–1988*, Macmillan, 1992.

45 Payne, P.L., 'Industrial entrepreneurship and management in Great Britain, c.1760–1970', *Cambridge Economic History of Europe*, Vol. VII, Cambridge University Press, Cambridge, 1978.

46 Perkin, H., *The Rise of Professional Society*, Routledge, 1989.

47 Pollard, S., *The Development of the British Economy, 1914–1980*, Arnold, 1983.

48 Pollard, S., *Britain's Prime and Britain's Decline*, Arnold, 1989.

49 Pope, R. (ed.), *Atlas of British Social and Economic History since 1700*, Routledge, 1989.

50 Rubinstein, W.D., *Capitalism, Culture and Decline in Britain, 1750–1990*, Routledge, 1993.

51 Sanderson, M., *The Universities and British Industry, 1850–1970*, Routledge & Kegan Paul, 1972.

52 Stephens, M.D., *Universities, Education and the National Economy*, Routledge, 1989.

53 Supple, B. (ed.), *Essays in Business History*, Oxford University Press, Oxford, 1977.

54 Supple, B., 'Fear of failing: economic history and the decline of Britain', *Economic History Review*, 2nd series, 47: 3, pp. 441–58, August 1994.

55 Tomlinson, J., *Public Policy and the Economy since 1900*, Oxford University Press, Oxford, 1990.

56 Wiener, M., *English Culture and the Decline of the Industrial Spirit*, Cambridge University Press, Cambridge, 1981.

General works covering the period before 1939

57 Aldcroft, D.H., *The Inter-War Economy: Britain 1919–1939*, Batsford, 1970.

58 Aldcroft, D.H. and Richardson, H.W., *The British Economy, 1870–1939*, Macmillan, 1969.

59 Alford, B.W.E., *Depression and Recovery? British Economic Growth, 1918–1939*, Macmillan, 1972.

60 Berghoff, H. and Möller, R., 'Tired pioneers and dynamic newcomers? A comparative essay on English and German entrepreneurial history, 1870–1914', *Economic History Review*, 2nd series, 47: 2, pp. 262–87, May 1994.

61 Booth, A., 'Britain in the 1930s: a managed economy?', *Economic History Review*, 2nd series, 40: 4, pp. 499–522, November 1987.

62 Booth, A., 'Britain in the 1930s: a managed economy? A reply to Peden and Middleton', *Economic History Review*, 2nd series, 42: 4, pp. 548–56, November 1989.

63 Broadberry, S.N., *The British Economy Between the Wars, a Macro-economic Survey*, Blackwell, Oxford, 1986.

64 Broadberry, S.N., 'The emergence of mass unemployment: explaining macro-economic trends during the trans-World War I period', *Economic History Review*, 2nd series, 43: 2, pp. 271–82, May 1990.

65 Buxton, N.K. and Aldcroft, D.H. (eds), *British Industry Between the Wars*, Scolar, 1979.

66 Capie, F., *Depression and Protectionism: Britain between the Wars*, Allen and Unwin, 1983.

67 Capie, F. 'Effective protection and economic recovery in Britain, 1932–37', *Economic History Review*, 2nd series, 44: 2, pp. 339–42, May 1991.

68 Dowie, J.A., 'Growth in the inter-war period: some more arithmetic', *Economic History Review*, 2nd series, 21: 1, pp. 93–112, April 1968.

69 Edgerton, D.E.H. and Horrocks, S.M., 'British industrial research and development before 1945', *Economic History Review*, 2nd series, 47: 2, pp. 213–38, May 1994.

70 Eichengreen, B.J. and Hatton, T.J., *Inter-war Unemployment in International Perspective*, Kluwer Academic, Dordrecht, 1988.

71 Feinstein, C.H., 'Britain's overseas investments in 1913', *Economic History Review*, 2nd Series, 43: 2, pp. 288–95, May 1990.

72 Floud, R. and McCloskey, D. (eds), *The Economic History of Britain since 1700*, Vol. II, *1860–1939*, Cambridge University Press, Cambridge, 1994.

73 Garside, W.R., *British Unemployment 1919–1939*, Cambridge University Press, Cambridge, 1990.

74 Greasley, D. and Oxley, L., 'Discontinuities in competitiveness: the impact of the First World War on British industry', *Economic History Review*, 2nd series, 49: 1, pp. 82–100, February 1996.

75 Kitson, M., Solomou, S. and Weale, M., 'Effective protection and economic recovery in the United Kingdom during the 1930s', *Economic History Review*, 2nd series, 44: 2, pp. 328–38, May 1991.

76 McCloskey, D.N. (ed.), *Enterprise and Trade in Victorian Britain*, Allen and Unwin, 1981.

77 Middleton, R., 'Britain in the 1930s: a managed economy?', *Economic History Review*, 2nd series, 42: 4, pp. 544–47, November 1989.

78 Payne, P.L., *British Entrepreneurship in the Nineteenth Century*, Macmillan, 1974.

79 Peden, G.C., 'Britain in the 1930s: a managed economy?', *Economic History Review*, 2nd series, 42: 4, pp. 538–43, November 1989.

80 Pollard, S. (ed.), *The Gold Standard and Employment Policies Between the Wars*, Methuen, 1970.

81 Ross, D., 'Commercial banking in a market-orientated financial system: Britain between the wars', *Economic History Review*, 2nd series, 49: 2, pp. 314–35, May 1996.

82 Sanderson, M., 'The English civic universities and the industrial spirit, 1870–1914', *Historical Research*, 61: 144, pp. 90–104, February 1988.

83 Simon, B., *Education and the Labour Movement, 1870–1920*, Lawrence and Wishart, 1974.

General works covering the period after 1939

84 Alford, B.W.E., *British Economic Performance, 1945–1975*, Cambridge University Press, Cambridge, 1995.

85 Barnett, C., *The Audit of War*, Macmillan, 1986.

86 Cairncross, A., *Years of Recovery. British Economic Policy 1945–51*, Methuen, 1985.

87 Cairncross, A., *The British Economy since 1945*, Blackwell, Oxford, 1992.

88 Central Statistical Office, *Fighting with Figures*, HMSO, 1995.

89 Crafts, N.F.R., and Woodward, N. (eds), *The British Economy since 1945*, Oxford University Press, Oxford, 1991.

90 Dow, J.C.R., *The Management of the British Economy, 1945–60*, Cambridge University Press, Cambridge, 1964.

91 Edgerton, D.E.H., 'The prophet militant and industrial: the peculiarities of Correlli Barnett', *Twentieth-Century British History*, 2, pp. 360–79, 1991.

92 Floud, R. and McCloskey, D. (eds), *The Economic History of Britain since 1700*, Vol. III, *1939–1992*, Cambridge University Press, Cambridge, 1994.

93 Hancock, W.K. and Gowing, M., *British War Economy*, HMSO, 1949.

94 Harrison, M., 'Resource mobilisation for World War II: the U.S.A, U.K., U.S.S.R. and Germany, 1938–1945', *Economic History Review*, 2nd series, 41: 2, pp. 171–92, May 1988.

95 Matthews, R.C.O., 'Why has Britain had full employment since the war', *Economic Journal*, 78, pp. 555–69, 1968.

96 Pope, R., 'British demobilisation, 1941–46', unpublished PhD thesis, Lancaster University, 1986.

97 Postan, M.M., *British War Production*, HMSO and Longman, Green, 1952.

98 Robinson, E., *The New Polytechnics*, Penguin edn, Harmondsworth, 1968.

99 Tomlinson, J., 'Inventing "decline": the falling behind of the British economy in the postwar years', *Economic History Review*, 2nd series, 49: 4, pp. 731–57, November 1996.

100 Worswick, G.D.N. and Ady, P. (eds), *The British Economy 1945–50*, Oxford University Press, Oxford, 1952.

101 Worswick, G.D.N. and Ady, P. (eds), *The British Economy in the Nineteen Fifties*, Oxford University Press, Oxford, 1962.

Works dealing with particular industries

102 Ashworth, W., *The History of the British Coal Industry*, Vol. V, *1946–1982: The Nationalised Industry*, Oxford University Press, Oxford, 1986.

103 Bowden, S., 'Credit facilities and the growth of consumer demand for electric appliances in the 1930s', *Business History*, 32: 1, pp. 52–75, January 1990.

104 Bowden, S., 'Demand and supply constraints in the inter-war UK car industry: did the manufacturers get it right?', *Business History*, 33: 2, pp. 241–67, April 1991.

105 Boyns, T., 'Strategic responses to foreign competition: the British coal industry and the 1930 Coal Mines Act', *Business History*, 32: 3, pp. 133–45, July 1990.

106 Buxton, N.K., *The Economic Development of the British Coal Industry*, Batsford, 1978.

107 Church, R.A., *The Rise and Decline of the British Motor Industry*, Cambridge University Press, Cambridge, 1994.

108 Farnie, D.A., 'The textile machine-making industry and the world market, 1870–1960', *Business History*, 32: 4, pp. 150–65, October 1990.

109 Foreman-Peck, J., Bowden, S. and McKinlay, A., *The British Motor Industry*, Manchester University Press, Manchester, 1995.
110 Higgins, D.M., 'Rings, mules and structural constraints in the Lancashire textile industry, c.1945–c.1965', *Economic History Review*, 2nd series, 46: 2, pp. 342–62, May 1993.
111 Kirby, M.W., *The British Coalmining Industry, 1870–1946: A Political and Economic History*, Macmillan, 1977.
112 Lorenz, E.H., *Economic Decline in Britain. The Shipbuilding Industry 1890–1970*, Oxford University Press, Oxford, 1991.
113 McCloskey, D.N., *Economic Maturity and Entrepreneurial Decline: British Iron and Steel, 1870–1913*, Harvard University Press, Cambridge, Mass., 1973.
114 Musson, A.E., *Enterprise in Soap and Chemicals: Joseph Crosfield & Sons Limited 1815–1965*, Manchester University Press, Manchester, 1965.
115 Pollard, S. and Robertson, P.L., *The British Shipbuilding Industry, 1890–1914*, Harvard University Press, Cambridge, Mass., 1979.
116 Reader, W.J., *Imperial Chemical Industries: A History*. Vol. I, *The Forerunners 1870–1926*, and Vol. II, *The First Quarter-Century 1926–1952*, Oxford University Press, 1970, 1975.
117 Robson, R., *The Cotton Industry in Britain*, Macmillan, 1957.
118 Robertson, A.J., 'Lancashire and the rise of Japan, 1910–1937', *Business History*, 32: 4, pp. 87–105, October 1990.
119 Rose, M.B., 'International competition and strategic response in the textile industries since 1870', *Business History*, 32: 4, pp. 1–8, October 1990.
120 Sandberg, *Lancashire in Decline*, Ohio State University Press, Columbus, Ohio, 1974.
121 Singleton, J., 'Planning for cotton, 1945–51', *Economic History Review*, 2nd series, 43: 1, pp. 62–78, February 1990.
122 Singleton, J., 'Showing the white flag: the Lancashire cotton industry, 1945–65', *Business History*, 32: 4, pp. 129–49, October 1990.
123 Singleton, J., *Lancashire on the Scrapheap*, Oxford University Press, 1991.
124 Supple, B., *The History of the British Coal Industry*, Vol. IV, *1913–46: The Political Economy of Decline*, Oxford University Press, Oxford, 1987.

INDEX

References in italics indicate Glossary entries

RELATED TITLES

Paul Adelman, *The Rise of the Labour Party 1880–1945*
Third Edition (1996)   0 582 29210 7

'... remains one of the best works on synthesis of current historical interpretations on this subject.'

Teaching History

This popular study covers the formation of the Labour Party and its emergence as the main rival to the Conservatives. Dr Adelman examines the alternative explanations and concludes that while there is a consensus about the reasons for the creation of the Labour Party there is no agreement about why it rose to such prominence.

Stuart Ball, *The Conservative Party and British Politics 1902–1951*
(1995)   0 582 0800 2

'Stuart Ball has produced a book of value to anyone interested in exploring the historical roots of current arguments, and one which is highly recommended.'

Polity Scene

These were years of crisis for the Conservative Party – from bitter divisions over policy (for example over Joseph Chamberlain's tariff reform campaign before 1914), to electoral disasters in 1906 and 1945 and parliamentary revolts. Yet after each setback it soon recovered. This is a lucid account of a turbulent period in the history of what has been one of the most durable and adaptive forces in British politics.

Paul Adelman, *The Decline of the Liberal Party 1910–1031*
Second Edition (1995)   0 582 27733 7

In 1906 the Liberals were returned to power in a landslide victory and formed one of the most brilliant and constructive administrations in the history of twentieth-century Britain. Thereafter, however, the party went into a decline from which it has never really recovered. Paul Adelman's *Decline of the Liberal Party* seeks to explain why and how this dramatic transformation took place. First published in 1981 the book has proved itself one of the most useful, concise accounts of this phenomenon.

Kevin Jeffreys, *The Attlee Governments 1945–1951*
(1992)   0 582 06105 9

In 1945 the Labour government under Clement Attlee set about a major transformation of British society. In his succinct but comprehensive study, Dr Jeffreys analyses the main changes and relates them to debates within the Labour Party on the nature of its aims and how best to achieve them. He relates his analysis to a wide range of documentary material drawn from the ever increasing volume of primary sources for the period.

Andrew Boxer, *The Conservative Governments 1951–1964*
(1996)   0 582 20913 7

'... not only informative but also remarkably interesting too... This is a very good book.'

History Review

The 1950s was a period of unprecedented growth at home, but it also witnessed Britain's diminishing influence on the world stage, with growing dependence on the US, the withdrawal from Empire and failure to join the European Community. Based on the latest research, this book provides fresh analysis of these events and assesses the political record of the four consecutive Conservative premierships who brought these changes about.

Alex May, *Britain and Europe since 1945*
(1998)   0 582 30778 3

This is a succinct, timely introduction to one of the most fundamental and highly charged political questions which have dominated British politics since 1945: Britain's position in Europe. The author's chronological, rather than thematic, approach brings clarity to what is an enormously complex topic. The study traces the evolution of British policy towards Europe since 1945, presenting the full international context as well as the impact on domestic party politics – including an analysis of the divisions in the Conservative Party under John Major. Dr May considers the effect on the economic as well as the political life of Britain; explores the impact on her commonwealth and Atlantic partners, as well as other EC members; and examines the development of EC policy.

Stephen Constantine, *Unemployment in Britain between the Wars*
(1980)   0 582 35232 0

Drawing on a range of contemporary evidence, Stephen Constantine studies the nature and causes of unemployment in Britain during the 1920s and 1930s, and analyses the failure of successive inter-war governments to make a constructive response. He examines the state of the British economy in this period and assesses the impact of the world economic crisis of 1929–31 in both human and economic terms.

to be returned on or before
stamped below.